teach yourself®

amateur theatre
nicholas gibbs

For UK order enquiries: please contact Bookpoint Ltd, 130 Milton Park, Abingdon, Oxon, OX14 4SB. Telephone: +44 (0) 1235 827720. Fax: +44 (0) 1235 400454. Lines are open 09.00–17.00, Monday to Saturday, with a 24-hour message answering service. Details about our titles and how to order are available at www.teachyourself.co.uk

For USA order enquiries: please contact McGraw-Hill Customer Services, PO Box 545, Blacklick, OH 43004-0545, USA. Telephone: 1-800-722-4726. Fax: 1-614-755-5645.

For Canada order enquiries: please contact McGraw-Hill Ryerson Ltd, 300 Water St, Whitby, Ontario, L1N 9B6, Canada. Telephone: 905 430 5000. Fax: 905 430 5020.

Long renowned as the authoritative source for self-guided learning – with more than 50 million copies sold worldwide – the **teach yourself** series includes over 500 titles in the fields of languages, crafts, hobbies, business, computing and education.

British Library Cataloguing in Publication Data: a catalogue record for this title is available from the British Library.

Library of Congress Catalog Card Number: on file.

First published in UK 2007 by Hodder Education, 338 Euston Road, London, NW1 3BH.

First published in US 2007 by The McGraw-Hill Companies, Inc.

This edition published 2007.

The **teach yourself** name is a registered trade mark of Hodder Headline.

Typeset by Transet Limited, Coventry, England.
Printed in Great Britain for Hodder Education, a division of Hodder Headline, an Hachette Livre UK Company, 338 Euston Road, London, NW1 3BH, by Cox & Wyman Ltd, Reading, Berkshire.

The publisher has used its best endeavours to ensure that the URLs for external websites referred to in this book are correct and active at the time of going to press. However, the publisher and the author have no responsibility for the websites and can make no guarantee that a site will remain live or that the content will remain relevant, decent or appropriate.

Hachette's policy is to use papers that are natural, renewable and recyclable products and made from wood grown in sustainable forests. The logging and manufacturing processes are expected to conform to the environmental regulations of the country of origin.

Impression number   10 9 8 7 6 5 4 3 2 1
Year   2012 2011 2010 2009 2008 2007

contents

dedication

This Book is dedicated to my family, Gaynor, Stevanie and Skye.

It is also dedicated to the community theatre family for whom it is written.

acknowledgements

First, I would like to thank former National Operatic and Dramatic Association (NODA) Chief Executive Mark Pemberton, whose idea this book was, for giving me the commission. Second, I would like to thank my very, very patient and tolerant publisher Victoria Roddam at Hodder Education, editor Vicky Butt and proofreader Jo Kemp.

I would also like to express my gratitude to everyone I met and corresponded with in researching and writing this book. Not everyone is mentioned in these pages simply because it was almost literally a cast of hundreds who passed on their knowledge and gave their opinions.

I would like to mention by name, however, Jane Dickerson (www.amdram.co.uk), Julie Petrucci (Combined Actors), Diana Mortimer and Rich Unwin (Peterborough Mask Theatre), Edward and Hilary Matty (West Bromwich Operatic Society), Meg Bray, Geoffrey Holme, Martin Roche, Mina Kirkbright, Cyril Hines, Sue Mooney and John Smeathers (Greater Manchester Drama Festival), Mike Linham (All-England Theatre Festival), Paul Taylor (Samuel French Ltd), Ian Reeder (Josef Weinberger Limited), Alan Baker (Penguin Club), Marie and Hedley O'Sullivan (St Ursula Players), Edward Turner and Sarah Coulson (Bramley Parish Theatre Players), John Ghent, Christine Hewson and everyone at Leicester Little Theatre, Pat Squires and Wallace Wareham (King's Theatre/NOMADS) and Melanie Ewles.

I hope that everyone's knowledge contained in these pages will help you as either a newcomer or as someone already involved in the world of community theatre.

part

one
community theatre:
getting involved

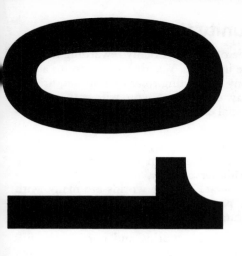

01

community theatre

In this chapter you will learn:
- how and when to join a community theatre group
- how to recognize a good community theatre group
- what is the commitment and cost of community theatre.

What is community theatre?

Community theatre is one of the most richly rewarding hobbies in which you can become involved. Whether you want to act or undertake one of the many non-acting roles that are required in the production of a play or musical, you will gain creative satisfaction and a new social circle that can draw on all sections of society.

In producing a play or musical you will be creating a unique world with each production. Plays can be set in history, the future, the present, in another country, on another planet or even in an alternative universe. Theatre worlds are many, with genres that range from pantomime to opera, which can be anything from a dark, brutal tragedy to a hilarious farce.

It is a chance to create different worlds and portray the full gamut of emotions. Where else could you be a lover, murderer, victim, singer, detective, inventor, Dad, Mum, lion, clown, three thousand years old or a toddler? And there are a lot more roles besides these.

Where else could you wear glorious gowns or sackcloth? Where else could you be the brave hero or the dastardly villain? Where else would you end up with the girl (or guy) after performing daring feats, engage in dramatic battles, fight demons (actual and metaphorical), have a different hairstyle, make a stand or die, but still be fit again the following evening to die all over again? And for all this, providing everything has gone well, you will be appreciated and applauded by a paying audience.

Actors are asked to create believable characters, but the world they inhabit has to be realized by a creative team combining the practical and artistic talents of a theatre group. Theatre only works with an audience and so you have to attract people to see and appreciate your efforts. Produce a good show and those people will return, allowing you to create and play in yet another world.

If you're technically minded, there are opportunities to develop skills in lighting, sound and special effects, all of which enhance the quality of production, giving the newly created world texture and mood, and delighting the senses of the audience.

You may wish to become a director and lead your group into your vision of a play, bringing together the wealth of talent at your disposal to realize something wonderful, giving satisfaction to performers, creatives and technicians alike, while giving an audience a thoroughly enjoyable evening's entertainment that can make them laugh, cry or spark a thought-provoking discussion.

Tap into your own creativity, with the only restriction being your own imagination (and, of course, the budget – but that is when you will be at your satisfying best, after creating an opulent prop for next to nothing!). Everyone is truly interdependent on everyone else, a team with no one working in isolation (if someone is, then something is wrong!). Any experience is welcome, but no experience is required – only a desire to listen, learn, share and enjoy.

From village halls to magnificent theatres, or even an open-air space, there are places calling you to create a world and/or perform for other people's pleasure and entertainment – and the richly rewarding pleasure for yourself.

This book is aimed at both the newcomer and those already involved in community theatre, proposing good advice and good practice to make the whole event of putting on plays an enjoyable one for everyone.

The world you are going to enter is a very popular one, with an estimated 440,000 people actively involved in Britain, around 2,500 affiliated amateur companies, their work entertaining a cumulative audience of over 7.5 million people paying a combined box-office turnover of a staggering £34 million. It is a world that has been a stepping stone for stars of the future, including the likes of Brenda Blethyn, Robbie Williams and Catherine Zeta-Jones.

Is it a time-consuming hobby?

To be involved in community theatre requires commitment and, as the old adage goes, what you get out of it depends on what you put into it. Although the end production may normally run for one or two weeks, there is great deal of preparation required by all those involved.

Generally speaking, actors will be required to rehearse two evenings a week over a three- or four-month period, with rehearsals increasing in frequency and intensity towards the end of the period. Musicals may require a longer period of rehearsal, while theatre-owning societies may have a much shorter and more intense rehearsal period (four or five times a week for fewer weeks). Aside from that, there is the 'homework' of learning lines plus the additional time required for costume fittings and publicity.

Other backstage tasks can vary in duration but all work to the same deadline, whether the task is set building or sourcing and/or making props and costumes, creating publicity material and so on. For a Christmas production in December, work can begin as early as June with a series of pre-production meetings and, depending on your position within the production, could mean you are involved from that moment or, alternatively, you may not be required until the get-in (when the theatre group takes over the theatre for their production) as part of the backstage crew or front-of-house team.

In addition, of course, there is the social aspect. Community theatre groups attract a diverse range of people from different backgrounds and occupations, all of whom love to socialize, whether it be a drink in the pub after rehearsal or particular social events arranged by the society for its membership.

Is it going to be expensive?

No. The only cost to you would be an annual membership subscription. Although these vary from group to group, they tend not to be wildly expensive but will be compulsory if you were to participate in any of the group's productions or events.

Other costs may be incurred depending on the group's policy on such matters, for example, some groups charge an audition fee. Others ask actors to buy their own scripts if they are cast in a production. There are some societies that ask for a rehearsal fee, like a weekly subscription, which may go towards the cost of the rehearsal venue.

All groups should be explicit about the fees they charge and as such you must decide whether these are acceptable to you before you join any group.

The only other costs to you as a member may be for social or special events, to pay for your meal or contribute to the hiring of a hall or a professional tutor for a workshop, or a course or theatre trip. These types of event are optional and it will be your choice whether your wish to participate in this aspect of community theatre life.

Can community theatre be a starting point to becoming a professional?

There is a myriad of drama schools and courses of varying quality which, if you choose carefully and have the money to spend, should provide comprehensive training to be a professional actor. Unfortunately, none of these schools or courses can guarantee you a career as an actor. They probably could guarantee a career as an out-of-work actor, given the high level of unemployment in this very competitive business.

Community theatre can provide an unlikely course to professionalism, however. Actors such as Blenda Blethyn and Catherine Zeta-Jones both began in amateur societies before someone recognized their talent and paid them a wage for doing their hobby!

The advantage of being involved in a community theatre group for actors, both trained and untrained, is that they are applying the skills they need to be a professional actor. Acting is very much a 'doing' activity and the more you do it, the more you improve. There are some trained actors who refuse to get involved with community theatre, leaving dedicated amateur actors to gain more experience than the 'trained' professional. There is an immense wealth of talent and experience in community theatre which is well worth learning from.

Build up a portfolio of everything you've done in the theatre, including reviews and photographs, and this could help you if you should decide to make the step into a professional career.

The bottom line is, however, amateur actors are actors with better-paid jobs and it may be more satisfying and secure to be a member of a community theatre group than an unemployed trained actor whose next job is likely to be in telesales or as a waiter!

Do I need training to be anything other than an actor?

One of the most wonderful aspects of community theatre groups, invariably, is that there's always someone who knows something about any aspect of theatre – directing, stage managing, lighting, sound, set building and so on. If you don't want to be an actor but are interested in one of the other roles, most theatre groups offer the opportunity to get involved. Unless you have experience of a given role you are unlikely to walk straight into it, but any theatre group worth its salt will give you the chance to be mentored by someone within the group in your area of interest. In addition, there are courses and workshops run by organizations such as NODA (National Operatic and Dramatic Association) and at theatres or by local colleges, where practical experience may be gained.

Certainly, if one member of a group does not know about a particular aspect of theatre they will know whom to ask within the group. That person in turn will point you in the right direction. Indeed, any new member expressing an interest in any non-acting capacity will be welcomed with open arms and positively encouraged. Specialist backstage people are worth their weight in gold and if your inclination is not to go on stage but you still want to be involved, any theatre group will welcome you and cherish your membership and contribution.

What are the signs of a good company?

The first outward sign of a good theatre group is the quality of the productions. If you have the chance, go and see a production of the group in which you are interested. If you are impressed and are still interested, talk to any members who may be present at the venue and see how welcoming they are and learn more about their activities.

Seeing a production is not always easy as the majority of community theatre groups average two productions a year. In this digital age most groups have a website and it is worth visiting. You will be able to check out what kind of productions they do, what kind of reviews they have been receiving and what opportunities there may be within the group. There should be a contact email address and it is worth asking questions about the group although, to be honest, you will not really know whether you wish to spend time with this group of people until you meet them for the first time.

If you are interested in joining as an actor it is worth examining cast lists from the most recent productions. If the same people are always in the lead roles you should consider why this is. It may be that the group has too few members. If so, why is this? Or it may be that the group has stagnated and cast within their comfort zone. If so, do you really want to join a group where opportunity is limited?

Are some companies more 'professional' than others?

The truth is that the standard of community theatre has improved immensely. This is borne out of necessity because any potential audience member always has other attractions to go to and spend their hard-earned money on, so productions have to be of a decent standard. The best community theatre groups can blur the distinction between amateur and professional with the sheer quality of their productions.

The 'professional' attitude stems from the passion and commitment of the group and the individuals within it. The 'it doesn't matter we're only amateur' attitude is on the wane and people involved in community theatre do not deliberately set out to make bad theatre or give the audience a poor experience.

However, be wary of the theatre group that is driven by one or two individuals who write and direct everything. The chances are that those groups are stagnating because no one has challenged the quality of the work they are doing as the individuals concerned regard the group as 'their' theatre company and may embark on vanity projects that would be more about them than the audience.

When is the best time to join a theatre group?

The best time to join is in the build-up to a production. You will be welcomed and the chances are you will be asked to become involved in some way with the production team. There is much to do to get a play on stage and theatre groups never believe they have enough people to do it.

The advantage here is that you are able actually to meet and mix with the other members of the group and gain a little bit of experience. Of course, the production culminates with an end-of-show party where you will meet pretty well everyone else – warts and all!

But don't wait for an up and coming production. If you're interested, contact the group – they may hold other social or workshop events or play readings that you could attend and from which you could learn more about the group.

02

the actors

In this chapter you will learn:
- what an actor does
- how to become an actor
- how to develop basic acting skills.

What is an actor?

Put simply, an actor is someone who plays a character in a scripted (occasionally improvised) play. An actor should be able to transform himself or herself from who they are in real life into a completely different fictional character – through the way they walk, talk and dress, and through their gestures.

How do I get a part in a play?

The vast majority of people join drama groups to be actors. Most groups will accept you as a member irrespective of your acting experience. Even if you have never set foot on a stage before, or least not since the Primary School nativity play, you will be welcomed and groups will encourage and help you to set foot on stage in character with confidence.

Societies have differing policies regarding new members and acting opportunities. There are those that operate on the basis of having you serve a kind of apprenticeship, with the best you can hope for being a small non-speaking role. (If you have never acted before, this may be a good opportunity for you to gain confidence for going on stage in front of an audience.) Others have a more open policy that offers opportunities for everyone and, if they think you are right for the part, would be willing to cast you in a leading role.

The ways in which acting roles are normally determined for a production are through a process called auditions. You will be asked to fill in a form giving your details, indicating what roles you wish to be considered for and detailing your availability. Since this new hobby primarily takes place in the evenings and in your own time, your work and/or home life might make you unavailable at certain times or on certain dates, for example, if you are going holiday or attend an evening class on a certain weekday evening. Note those dates down on the form as this helps the director to draw up an appropriate rehearsal schedule that can accommodate your needs.

You can express on your form that you only want a small part or even a non-speaking part in a play. Alternatively, you may jump straight in and go for one of the principal roles.

The audition

For the audition you will be asked to read and act from a pre-selected audition piece from the play. You should be able to get a copy of the audition piece before the actual audition so that you can prepare yourself. Try and read the play at least once so you do know for what kind of show you are auditioning. If possible, try and memorize the audition piece because this will allow you to give a better performance. Treat the audition as a performance because it may be the only opportunity you have to play the part.

You may be asked to audition alongside several different people. On each occasion give your best because any one of those people could be in the cast with you. The director will be looking for the best combination of people for the cast and not necessarily who you like best!

You will usually be asked to perform the audition piece before the director and two or three other people from his/her creative team. This can be nerve-racking for some people, but the director and his/her team will understand. Remember, they will want you to give a good performance to make the casting of the play as hard as possible for them. Directors love choice.

If competition is fierce for a particular role, you may be called back for a second or third audition. Once the auditions are complete, there are three possibilities:

- You will be cast in the role you coveted.
- You will be cast in another role in the play.
- You will not be cast at all.

Although the third scenario is disappointing, do not despair. There are many reasons why directors cast a play the way they do, but not getting a role in this play will not prevent you getting a role in future productions.

The director has many factors to consider, including a balanced cast. A football analogy is helpful here. Wayne Rooney is one of the best footballers in the world, but if the manager decided to field 11 Rooneys, despite the abundance of talent, the team would be rubbish. Different skills are needed for different roles and this is particularly applicable in theatre. Leading actor A may be the best thing ever, but if he doesn't look right or work well with leading actress B, also fantastic, then the play won't work. There could be any number of reasons for failure at audition and this should not prevent you treading the boards in the next production.

If you have been successful and are given a part you will be presented with a script (some societies ask you to buy the script). The next step is to learn your part and attend rehearsals.

The read-through

The first rehearsal will probably be a read-through, which all the cast and crew attend. Here you will meet the whole production team. The read-through can be beneficial for actors because they may be able to try out a few ideas for delivery of their lines and get some idea of how other actors are approaching their parts. Be warned, however, some actors don't commit to any form of interpretation at the read-through but merely read the script aloud. This isn't necessarily a bad thing but just the way some actors approach their roles.

Learning the part

Learning the part you have been allocated is not just about learning lines (of which more below). You have to learn to become someone else. In basic terms, the actor becomes the character. But how do you become the character?

Read the script

To become the character, you have to understand the person you want to portray. The only way to do this is to ask questions when reading the script. For major roles, all the information an actor needs to know about his character is in the script. The basic questions you need to ask are:

- Who am I?
- What do I want?
- Why do I want it?
- What is the situation?
- How can I achieve what I want?

Within the script you will find all the necessary biographical information about your character and also what can be inferred from the script (sub-text). A useful task is to write down everything you can discover about your character from the script, ranging from factual information (e.g. he is a Captain in the army); viewpoint (e.g. he hates being in the army); other opinions (e.g. many of the men in his command hate him, Private Smith calls him a 'drudge') and so on.

From that you will build up a picture of the kind of person you are meant to be portraying and sense the character's state of mind and their emotions, both expressed and internal. Remember, however, that not everything said about and by your character is necessarily true, and recognize the falsehoods from the truth. The question to ask is why these falsehoods exist.

Find your character's motivation

While reading, you should always ask why your character does anything. What is the motivation? If you can come up with an answer each time, you will understand the character in the moment on stage.

Every major character will have an overall goal they want to achieve. Identify what that is and why your character wants to achieve that goal, for example, the mother who wants to stop her daughter marrying a young upstart who she thinks is below her class, or the professor who wants to take over the world to save mankind.

What obstacles are in the way to prevent your character from reaching that goal? Does your character overcome those obstacles and achieve the goal? If the goal is not achieved, why is this? (e.g. The professor is thwarted by the hero.) Is the goal no longer relevant to your character at the end? (e.g. The young upstart turns out to be a decent chap.)

Motivation does not apply solely to the big things, but the banal things too. Why does the character go to the kitchen? Motivation: to make a cup of coffee. Why does he clean the blood from the carpet? Motivation: to remove evidence of the murder. Why does he kiss the girl? Motivation: love, desire or lust?

Talking to your fellow cast members and the director about your character and their characters will also help you.

Develop speech patterns

Remember when you are delivering your lines that you are doing so in your character's voice. The obvious example would be if your character speaks in a dialect or with an accent, although that is fraught with many dangers. A production featuring an Irish family with English actors can see all family members speaking with an Irish accent but not from the same part of Ireland! With accents and dialects, do get some coaching, preferably from someone who possesses the accent or dialect naturally.

On a more basic level, putting accents and dialects aside, there are speech patterns. Everyone speaks in their own idiosyncratic way, due to education, occupation, family, status and so on. The characters that you play may not have the same speech patterns as you. Your character may speak in short sentences or half sentences, others may ramble on, others may speak in a flowery, detailed way, or may have a particular speech tick where they repeat certain phrases like 'you know' or 'he said/she said'.

An often-heard cry from an amateur actor is that he/she can't say the lines because they are badly written. On occasions that may be true, but in the vast majority of cases it is because the actor cannot be bothered to play the character as written. Bear in mind that you need explicit permission from the playwright or their agent to make any changes to the script.

There is a rhythm to every speech pattern and the writer has deliberately written the lines in a particular way because it is what makes up the character's personality. Once you are familiar with the lines, their meaning and context, your speech will flow.

Learn your lines

Learning lines can be the most daunting job for a newcomer to the stage, before they even get to the actual acting. There are many techniques for learning lines and if you were to ask your fellow theatre group members you would end up with a list of different methods. At this point all I can say is that you will have to find the one that works for you. Techniques for learning lines include:

- learning line-by-line, going down the page with a ruler and reciting
- physically writing or typing out the lines
- recording the lines on to tape (or CD, i-Pod, MP3 player) and frequently listening to them
- reciting the lines whenever possible, be it in the shower or in the car
- simply reading and rereading the play over and over again.

Your character's body language

Various studies have revealed that approximately 7 per cent of human communication is achieved through the words we use; another 7 per cent is achieved through the way we say those words. The remaining 86 per cent is achieved through non-verbal means, that is, how we stand, gesture and move.

In creating a character, the way you stand and move is very important. For example, a military man would stand upright with his shoulders back, and would be disciplined in his movements. A pickpocket would be quick, subtle and nimble. The bullied school child may walk with his eyes to the ground and cower in the presence of others. On the assumption that the actors are probably not any of these in real life then they have to assume the stance and movement of such characters. This comes from observation of real people or the portrayal of similar characters on stage or screen.

This is equally important to minor characters, both speaking and non-speaking. The way you stand or move, whether you are a waiter, a guard or part of a crowd, has to be how a real waiter or guard would stand or move. The audience will notice if anyone is 'out of character'. Theatre is first and foremost a visual medium and 86 per cent of what anyone does on stage is communicated to the audience before a word is spoken.

Costume

Aside from rehearsals, the homework for learning lines and maybe researching your character, as an actor you will be required for measurements and costume fitting. You may not get your costume until very late in the rehearsal period – on occasions it may not be until the dress rehearsal – but try and become familiar with it, particularly if it involves wearing unfamiliar clothes and boots. This usually applies in historical dramas. Remember, your character has probably been wearing this type of clothing and footwear for years, so you have to look comfortable in it.

What an actor wears on stage is part of his/her character and, the chances are, you will be wearing clothes that you do not normally wear, particularly if the play is a period piece. The costume for which you have been measured to wear on stage will make a significant difference to the portrayal of your character, and unfamiliar footwear in particular will affect your movement. Wear your costume and footwear as often as you can so you feel comfortable and natural in them. In community theatre costumes often arrive late in the rehearsal process, so opportunities to familiarize yourself with your new garments will be short. Essentially, find out if you can do in your costume what you have been doing in rehearsals. Certainly mention to the wardrobe department any significant movements you do such as falling, swinging, saluting, fighting and so on.

Research

You may wish to research your character, their situation and their world to get a better understanding of the person you are playing. Research can be a useful thing if you are dealing with an unfamiliar time period and you wish to learn the correct etiquette of the time, or a character's political persuasions, or what was it like to be on a prison ship. It will add to your understanding of the character and their world. However, do not over-research to the point where it eclipses the type of character you're playing. In all characters it is the humanity that is important, their feelings and emotions and the empathy they have with the audience. Ultimately, everything you need to know should be in the script.

Rehearsals and preparation

The rehearsal period can vary in length depending on the production and on how each society works. A full-length play can take up to six months (usually four months) to rehearse, with one or two evening rehearsals a week. The frequency of rehearsals per week usually increases the closer you get to performance week. Some theatre-owning amateur companies can be staging up to 12 plays a year and in those cases the rehearsal period is shorter and more intense. A six-week production period can require the actors four or five times a week.

If you have a leading role or if the play is an ensemble work, you will be required for almost every rehearsal. If, however, you have a minor part you will only be required for rehearsals of the scenes in which your character appears. However, if possible, I would recommend you attend as many rehearsals as you can. It is a great way of learning more about acting and the various facets of production. Ask questions of the people who are there about what they are doing. The more you learn, the more comfortable you will become and, with the accumulated knowledge, the more valuable you will become to the group and you will have more options to choose from in future productions.

Rehearsals are about experimentation and repetition. You may work on scenes in various different ways until the best way is found. The repetition comes from doing the scene again and again until everything is perfect (or at least as good as it can be) for the performance.

Voice preparation

If you haven't done any acting before, it is important that you train your voice so that your words can be projected clearly, otherwise your hobby will be shouting in the evenings, which won't be a hobby for very long because you will damage your voice! It is all in the breathing and it is worth taking the time to do some breathing exercises to improve your projection.

Breathing exercise 1

Practise a controlled breathing exercise called the intercostal and diaphragmatic method, in which you inhale through the nose and exhale through the mouth. Deeply inhale and exhale in a controlled manner. When you inhale through the nose you will feel the lower ribs move upwards and outwards. Simultaneously the diaphragm – the muscle that separates the chest and lungs from the abdomen – will flatten and descend. If you place a hand on your abdomen you will feel this happening.

When you exhale through the mouth in a controlled manner the ribs and diaphragm will revert to their normal positions. What you are doing with this exercise is controlling your breathing, but when you do it avoid moving your shoulders, which is what often happens when people inhale through the mouth!

The exercise is further enhanced by increasing the length of time you take to exhale all your breath.

Breathing exercise 2

Add a vocal sound to exercise 1 and hold the sound until you have completely exhaled. It can be any vocal sound, such as a musical note or vowel sounds A, E, I, O, U. This will strengthen your voice and improve your projection, you will be less likely to damage your voice and all your words will be heard by all audience members – even those at the back!

Breathing exercise 3

The next step is to vary the range of vocal sounds you make so that your voice still carries the same force. Once you feel comfortable with the sounds you make in exercise 2, repeat the exercise but this time change the way you are making the vocal sounds, beginning with a low whisper and gradually increasing at your own pace until you produce a loud shout that isn't a strain on your voice. This will help strengthen the power and control of your voice and will ensure that everyone hears you clearly.

Do these breathing exercises daily, for about 10 minutes, and it will become second nature and, quite frankly, you will feel better for it too. A word of warning if you are doing the 'sound' exercises at home – tell your partner and/or family what you are doing or they will think you have gone mad!

Script, pencil and eraser

You will be allowed to keep the script in your hand during the early stages of rehearsal and the most important items to have with you will be a pencil with an eraser. With the pencil you will be expected to mark up any instructions from the director or for yourself, particularly entrances, exits and moves. The eraser is important because things may change and an earlier instruction may become irrelevant and replaced with something else.

There will be a clearly defined point, specified by the director before rehearsals begin, when all actors will put their scripts down. However, the earlier you can get the script out of your hand the better it will be for your overall acting.

Once you have memorized your lines you will work on their delivery. The way you say your lines will be affected by the way your fellow cast members deliver theirs, but if you already know your words, polishing an inflection or meaning here and there should not be a problem.

Blocking

During the first phase of rehearsals, most directors use a technique called 'blocking'. Essentially, blocking is the director's way of familiarizing the actors with the set, their position and movement on it, as well as entrances and exits. However, all these movements are provisional and some may change as rehearsals reveal better ways of doing things.

At this point it is worth becoming familiar with some of the basic theatrical terms regarding the performance area. You may be asked to move 'down stage' or exit 'stage left', etc. Below is a mini-glossary of what these mean.

downstage	The part of the stage that is closest to the audience.
stage left	On an actor's left side as he/she stands on the stage looking out to the audience.
stage right	On an actor's right side as he/she stands on the stage looking out to the audience.
upstage	The area of the stage that is furthest away from the audience.
wings	The areas either side of the stage, which should not be seen by members of the audience.

Cues

It is not just your own lines you should be aware of, but also the lines uttered by your fellow actors, particularly what is known as your cues. In essence, cues tell you when you are supposed to speak (and/or move and enter/exit) and they can come in the following forms:

- another actor's line, e.g. 'Answer the question, Gerald.'
- an actor's movement, e.g. Gerald rushes toward you
- a sound or music effect, e.g. a gun shot or the radio is heard
- a lighting change or visual effect, e.g. the stage lights dim to signify night.

You will need to note all these cues in your script and learn them. Failure to meet a cue can reduce the pace, tension and/or humour of a scene, which affects the enjoyment of the audience.

Listening

One of the most important aspects to acting is listening. On stage and in rehearsal you should always listen to what is being said and how it is being said by your fellow actors, and not just listen for your cues. Remember, on stage the events that are unfolding around your character are happening for the first time. They are new to the character and you must act/react accordingly. Acting is not just about the words you speak on stage but your character's reaction to sounds, sights and what is said by other characters.

The other thing about listening is that you understand what is going on, particularly if a cue has been missed or the script has skipped a couple of pages. You will have to react to the moment and find a way of getting back on track!

Scripts down

The director will set a date in the rehearsal schedule when he/she will expect all the actors to have learned their lines and be able to perform without referring to the script in their hand. This transition sees the security of having your lines in your hand disappear, and is the first steps from rehearsal to performance status.

Actors can struggle with this phase and may require prompting often, but as rehearsals without scripts progress the prompts should become fewer and, certainly by the dress rehearsal, be non-existent. You will be aware of how your performance changes for the better once the script is out of your hand.

Director's notes

During rehearsals, the director will give 'notes' to the cast. These notes are given to improve the performance of individuals and the collective group. Always listen to the notes that affect you and take them on board – on no account get upset about them. If these notes are delivered in an offensive way it is likely to be to do with the director's personality rather than the valid points they are trying to make. (By all means, after the play, do tell the director that he/she needs to improve the delivery of their notes to the cast and crew.)

Props

Props, or properties, are the objects that actors use during the course of the performance. As soon as props are made available during the rehearsal period, use them and become familiar with them. Usually, hand props are objects a character may have used for years and therefore their use would be second nature to him or her, so you must become familiar with them and know how they work, e.g. writing with a quill, using a lighter, holding a rifle, using a 1920s telephone.

Publicity

You will probably be required for a photographic publicity session for the print and online media. This session could be an additional day to the scheduled rehearsals. Occasionally, you may be asked to undertake an interview for press, radio and, if the society is really lucky, television.

Technical rehearsals

Technical rehearsals – hate 'em, hate 'em, hate 'em! But they are very necessary. The 'tech', as it is colloquially known, takes place in the theatre when the set is completed, with its doors and windows in place, and when lighting and sound effects are introduced. For actors this can often be a tedious, repetitive and long drawn-out session, but it is even longer for the technical crew. From the actors' point of view it is the time when they find out whether exits and entrances work, how long it takes (or how practical it is) to open a window, how they should move to fit in with a lighting change, or whether the time allowed for a costume change is long enough. If you encounter any problems during the tech, report them as soon as practicable to the stage manager, who will try to solve the problem for you.

Dress rehearsal

The dress rehearsal is an uninterrupted run through of the play. It is run as a performance in the theatre, usually in front of a small audience. Often in community theatre this will be the only opportunity for the play to run as it should before a paying audience attends the opening night. It is when you may become aware of glitches, which you will have to resolve before the following night. Make the stage manager aware of any problems in the dress rehearsal.

On the night

Arrival at the theatre

Actors should arrive at the theatre no later than the designated time specified by the stage manager and should sign in.

Arrival times will vary from actor to actor and will be determined by how much time they need in the make-up chair and how much time they need to get into their costume.

At the very least, no actor should arrive later than half an hour before curtain-up.

Checking costume, props and set

On arrival it is wise for actors first to check that their costume is present and complete in the dressing room – if not, contact a member of the wardrobe team immediately.

Actors should then check that all their hand props are where they should be – if not, contact a member of the props team immediately.

Re-familiarize yourself with the set before the audience comes into the auditorium, and check that everything is where it ought to be.

Preparing for performance

Actors, like sportsmen, prepare for a performance in very different ways, but all are geared to take control of their nerves.

Nerves

Before a performance you are going to be nervous. It is a perfectly natural reaction, but the trick is to control your nerves so they don't overwhelm you and lead to 'stage fright'.

- The first thing you can do on a performance day is not to think about the play until you arrive at the theatre.
- The source of nerves invariably focuses on what can go wrong: 'What if I forget my lines?' 'What if I lose the prop?' 'What if a meteor hits the theatre?' Mark Twain was quoted as saying: 'I have been through some terrible things in my life, some of which actually happened.' That is, things that people worry about almost never happen.
- Be positive. Think about the good things, such as that you were word perfect in rehearsal; you have a great supportive cast and crew; you have a great role. Visualize yourself receiving applause at the end of the night.

Warm-up

Physical and vocal warm-ups are highly recommended because they will help you relax and take your mind off the nerves!

Physical warm-up

The physical warm-up should take no more than ten minutes. Find a space to do the warm-up either on your own or with fellow cast members. The warm-up should, as if you were preparing to play sport or go jogging, be a series of stretching and shaking exercises which will relieve any tension in your muscles and get the blood flowing about your body (although your nerve-racked heart is already doing that with an increased heart rate).

Vocal warm-up

The vocal warm-up should include the breathing exercises you do at home, a facial stretching exercise such as an over-the-top chewing action, and perhaps a couple of tongue twisters.

Make-up

How much make-up you wear will depend on the role you are playing. It is likely that in your first few shows someone will apply basic make-up for you and soon you will be able to apply it yourself. If time and resources permit during the rehearsal period, see if you can practise applying your own make-up. However, if the creative team includes a make-up team, let them loose on your face, hair or any other part of your body because they will do an excellent job.

If your character needs a great deal of make-up then it should be left to an expert. Indeed, there could be varying degrees of experimentation required during the rehearsal period before the 'look' is established. The experimentation will determine how long you will need in the make-up chair and that in turn will determine when you need to arrive at the theatre.

Beginner's call

From about half an hour before curtain-up there will be a countdown, with the stage manager – or assistant stage manager – announcing that it is 30 minutes, 20 minutes, 10 minutes and 5 minutes to the start of the show. Finally, 'beginners please' will be announced and at that point all the actors in the opening scene need to take up their positions ready for the play to begin.

The bottom line is that it is the actor's responsibility to be in position, not just for the start of the play but for all subsequent entrances throughout the performance, so they have to be aware of what is going on on stage. Many theatres have a feedback microphone that broadcasts the play via loudspeaker in the dressing rooms. However, that is not always possible so close attention must be paid to the on-going performance.

The performance and afterwards

When the play is under way there may be unanticipated incidents – both welcome and unwelcome – during a performance. Below are some of the possible events and how the actor should react.

Drying – This is when an actor forgets their lines. In such circumstances it is important to maintain the momentum of the scene. If you realize you have forgotten you should ask quickly for a prompt and carry on. If one of your fellow cast members is guilty of drying it may be possible for you to help them out without the need of a prompt.

Laughter – Never speak through audience laughter but come in with your next line as the laughter is dying down. On no account wait for expected laughter as there is no guarantee it will come.

Applause in performance – On occasion audiences may give an actor or group of actors a round of applause for a particularly pleasing sequence. As with laughter, let the applause begin to subside before speaking your next line.

Gun does not fire – Guns on stage are erratic beasts and sometimes don't go 'bang!' In case this happens you should have a plan B for how to kill a character, or a witty retort, if no death or injury is scripted from the gunshot.

Missing prop – This is completely your own fault because you did not check it was where it should be. It may not be vital to the plot, but if it is, a convincing plan B is required.

Script jump – This is where an actor has taken up the wrong cue line and leapt several pages in the story. You will have to find a seamless way of getting back on track. Saying your correct line or speech next often does the trick.

Curtain call

At the end of the play, soak up the applause and perform the rehearsed curtain call in which you take your bows.

After the show

Before leaving the theatre or going to meet friends in the bar, make sure you remove your make-up and hang up and store your costume correctly in the dressing room. Make sure all your props are returned to the props team or are in their proper place.

Reviews

Read or listen to any theatre review with a pinch of salt. If you receive a good review, revel in it, of course, but if not, remember it is only one person's view (who hasn't bought a ticket, by the way) and what do they know about theatre anyway!

Last performance

After the last performance, once you have removed your make-up and costume, it is important that you help out with dismantling the set. The more people who help the faster it can be done. It may be part of the theatre's contract with the theatre group that the 'get-out' is completed by a given time or there could be financial penalties which will affect the group's box office.

The temptation is to go and see your friends in the bar, but if you explain to them in advance that you have to help with dismantling the set they will understand and, of course, wait for you.

Members should note if any actors suddenly become work-shy with convenient bad backs after the final curtain. It could prove a factor in casting for the next or future productions.

Ultimately, remember how many people, who do not seek the limelight, have worked hard to get you on stage. Helping them out on the final night will do wonders for your reputation within the group.

The run

Community theatre productions are usually short runs, with four to seven performances in a week being the norm. By the time you have managed to control your first-night nerves and are just getting into your acting stride the production has finished. Other amateur productions can have longer runs: popular musicals may run for a fortnight, and seasonal productions such as pantomimes may also have a longer run. At Tolethorpe near Stamford, Lincolnshire, the English Shakespeare Company has three on-going amateur productions that span a ten-week open-air summer season. Other amateur companies tour or take part in festivals, which can also extend the run.

Whenever the show ends, however, there is post-production euphoria (if all has gone well) followed by an empty feeling of sadness. This, no doubt, will spur you on to wanting to become involved in more productions.

Actors' dos and don'ts

Don'ts

Actors should not, under any circumstances:

- talk or whisper in the wings
- go outside the theatre wearing their costumes
- invite friends or family backstage
- have mobile phones, particularly mobile phones with cameras, switched on backstage
- play tricks on fellow cast members on stage, such as hiding props or deliberately changing lines
- upstage a fellow actor
- play to particular members of the audience, such as family and friends
- mimic another actor's speech – this, to be fair, is an unconscious thing where actors have learned the script so well they 'mouth' the other parts as well as speak their own; this may be picked up in rehearsals, in which case steps should be taken to prevent it
- shuffle their feet on stage (unless it is part of the character).

Dos

Actors should:

- learn their lines early
- learn their cues
- learn their moves
- be punctual
- check costume, props and set
- listen to the director

- remain in character until they are off stage and out of sight of the audience
- listen to their fellow actors on and off stage
- help dismantle the set
- enjoy themselves.

Case study

Making a debut

Actress Diana Mortimer recalls her first role in an open-air production of *A Midsummer Night's Dream*.

'First thing was Puck in *A Midsummer Night's Dream*. It was scary because I hadn't had to learn so many lines before. So I set about learning my lines as quickly as possible so I didn't have that panic of "my goodness" because I had quite a few long speeches and stuff. It was daunting, but I felt quite secure within the company because there was a bunch of very experienced people there that could help you along. The rehearsal schedules were well laid out; you knew what you were doing, where you were going and consequently felt that there was a really strong background to everything and you would be taken along in a process that was tried and tested. So it was just a matter of going home and learning your lines and thinking about your character.'

03

the director

In this chapter you will learn:
- what the director does
- how to become a director
- what makes a good director.

What is a director?

The director is the most influential and important member of any production. It will be his/her overall vision of the play that will determine the nature of the production. To be a director you have to develop a collective group consciousness with all those on and off stage. Your relationships with everyone have to be good, while at the same time you need to develop a thick skin because, quite frankly, no production in the history of theatre has ever gone 100 per cent smoothly and there will always be moments of moaning and stress with which the director will have to deal. You're responsible for casting and the overall look of the play. You need a creative and practical backstage team who should be free to contribute and offer ideas, but ultimately you have the final say.

The director has to be a good listener, be encouraging and tactful without over-inflating an actor's ego, be able to criticize constructively without destroying an actor's confidence. Similarly, the backstage creative team must be given encouragement and shown appreciation. They are the unsung heroes of any production, who never see the limelight but are so important to the production and the director's vision for it.

It is worth noting that the director is a relatively modern innovation in theatre, only having arrived on the scene in the late nineteenth century, but the role was quickly established as an all-important one, helped in no small way by the director-led art forms of cinema and television.

A good director will:

- be a leader
- be inspirational
- be enthusiastic
- possess artistic vision
- be open to, and welcome, new ideas
- be understanding of, and encouraging to, actors, designers and technicians
- have an understanding of theatre
- be excellent at people management
- be able to communicate clearly and positively
- know how to read a play and champion it
- respect the ideas and abilities of others
- be prepared to ask, and learn from, those with appropriate knowledge.

How do I become a director?

It is extremely unlikely that as a new member you will step into directing a major production, unless you have a proven track record with other theatre groups. If you are interested in directing then serve as an assistant director or stage manager where you can see at first-hand the director's role. Also, it is worth drawing on your experience of directors either as cast or crew member. Who was the most enjoyable to work with? Why was it an enjoyable experience? By the same token, what was the least enjoyable experience and why? Take the good things you've learned from directors and leave the bad things.

Many drama groups will offer opportunities to first-time directors by giving them a one-act play to direct for a festival or at a small venue. They will be mentored by an experienced director and, if successful, will be offered a further opportunity to direct a similar production on their own or, if very fortunate, be presented with a chance to direct a major production.

It is advisable to try and learn as much as you can about putting on a production and from the varied knowledge that many people possess within the drama group. Do not be afraid to ask questions even if you think they are silly. The more you know, the more comfortable you will feel as a director. Good directors may not know everything but they will know who to ask if they don't know something or need clarification.

The directing process

The process of directing a play has many stages, which see the director starting work on a play long before anyone else is involved. Here is a step-by-step guide to the director's role.

Choosing the play

The director and the play may come together by one of two methods. The first possibility it that you choose a play that you like and try to convince the drama group's committee that it will be a worthwhile project, either artistically or financially but preferably both. Alternatively, the committee may approach you about directing a particular play.

Director's rule No 1

Only direct a play that you are passionate about, because it is a big commitment and responsibility and you really want to work on something that is of interest to you. You will be with this play for a long time.

Reading and rereading

The first thing a director will have to do, once he/she has chosen or accepted a play to direct, is to read it (many, many times). What you have to do is:

- read the dialogue and hear the different voices
- understand the story – what the events are and why they happen
- understand the characters – who they are, what motivates them, what happens to them
- visualize the play and develop an idea of how you want to stage it – the set, the costume, the tone and so on.

Reading dialogue and hearing voices

Everything you need to know about the play, aside from the occasional plot-specific stage direction or prop, is all in the dialogue – character, plot, tone, everything. It is all about what comes out of people's mouths. Unlike books where the author can spend pages describing a character's inner turmoil, all the director has are the spoken words of the characters created by the playwright.

Nearly all of the information in the play has to come through the dialogue of the characters, so this must be conveyed in different ways. Two words from a man of few words can express more than a long speech by the most erudite of characters. As you read the play, you have to hear the different voices of the characters. The speech rhythms of those characters may differ from what you are used to (e.g. any Shakespearean character), but you have to hear and understand them.

It is important that you ask questions of the characters, plot and overall script. Each time you read the script, have a notebook beside you and make notes listing your ideas, doubts and thoughts about the clarity of the script. You will have to identify the key dramatic moments and the turning points in the play (e.g. the discovery of a revelatory letter, or the realisation that the husband has been unfaithful, or the argument that escalates to violence).

You will have to know the play inside out and feel enthusiastic about it. You will have to convey this to your committee, who will want to have full confidence in you, and to your actors, designers, technicians, in fact to everyone in the drama group and, of course, to the audience.

Director's rule No 2

Write down everything you know about each character, about the plot, the key turning points. If you don't understand something, note it down and pursue the question until it is answered.

Visualizing

It is crucial to remember when reading the script that you are taking the words from the page and putting them on the stage. Theatre is a 3-D visual medium – you will have to visualize what is going on and how to arrange your actors on the stage.

In all likelihood you will know the venue where the production is to be staged, so you will know the dimensions of the stage and the theatre. Context is all and a fundamental question should be, 'Is the play suitable for the venue?' Visualize the action taking place in that performance space. Will it work? Ask yourself the following:

• What is the tone of the play?
• How should it be lit?
• What is the era of the play?
• Can it be transposed into another time?
• Will the staging be simple or elaborate?
• Will the set be minimal or ostentatious?
• What should the characters look like?
• What are the strongest images in the play?

Assembling a creative backstage team

Ideally, before you engage the actors you will need to appoint a trusted creative backstage team. The backstage team are the unsung heroes of any production. They do not seek the limelight but they make a significant contribution to the style, tone and quality of the production. They are a group of people who will be with you from the start, once the committee has given the go ahead. Every member of this team should be encouraged to contribute and share their ideas, and their knowledge should be drawn upon. Your relationships with these people are very important and you should treat them with the utmost respect for they work very, very hard.

The key personnel are:

- stage manager
- set designer/builder – dynamics, exits/entrances, placing of furniture and immovable objects
- costume designer (wardrobe department)
- props designer
- lighting designer/engineer
- sound designer/engineer.

The stage manager

The most important appointment of the backstage team is that of the stage manager. For the director, a good stage manager is of vital importance and someone whom you must trust implicitly because, for the most part, they work on their own initiative. They need to be organized and have the respect of the other members of the society. The stage manager will keep you informed about anything to do with the production and will arrange appropriate meetings with the backstage creative team. They will rarely intervene in artistic matters but you should be able to trust them to tell you the truth and, once in the theatre, you must trust them to run the show on your behalf.

Working with your creative team

When dealing with your creative team you will first need to convey your vision of the production, and then allow the costume, set and props designers to come up with the ideas for how to make that happen. Ideas should be encouraged and should never be dismissed, but ultimately you make the final decision. The creative team will consult and work together, and if you allow them to let their creative juices flow they will always come up with a winner and will not mind that you turned down their other ideas.

Via the stage manager, the director should have regular meetings and updates regarding progress in all things creative. Encourage everyone to show you what they have done at any given stage because, if it looks like something you did not envisage or want, it is better to say so early on, before too much wasted work has gone into a particular unwanted direction and while things can still be changed.

Working with the technicians

Working with the sound and lighting technicians are similar processes: you tell them what you want and they will go away and make it happen. In the case of the sound designer, you should be able to hear their work and incorporate it into the rehearsal process to see if it works.

With lighting, you will not see the designer's work until the technical rehearsal at the earliest, but in meetings with him/her it is important to be clear about the effects you want. You won't need to know the technical specifications of the lighting, but be clear about what you want to achieve and determine whether it is feasible in the venue in which you are performing.

Assembling the cast

Once the key creative backstage team is in place, you then have to find the talent to go on stage.

Play reading

Not all directors do this, but I think it is a good idea. Hold an informal, open play reading of the play you intend to direct. Read the whole play, with each character read by several different actors throughout the play. It is a way for those actors who are interested to read the whole play before auditions and also gives you the opportunity to convey some of your ideas about the play – all of which will help a nervous bunch of actors.

Audition pieces

Before the auditions are held you will need several audition pieces – namely sections from the play that highlight a particular character or characters – and then make them available to all who are interested. It is also helpful to write a brief paragraph about each character, listing basic facts and traits about them.

Auditions

The first thing to do is to get every auditioning actor to fill out a form. The form should contain their name, contact details, what role they wish to audition for, whether they would be happy to be considered for an alternative role on stage or backstage and, most importantly, when they are available and unavailable (e.g. evening classes or holiday/work commitments).

For auditions it is important for the director to be joined by two or three people – e.g. stage manager and assistant director – from the creative team to offer their views on the candidates. Ideally have at least one person who is of the opposite sex because they may see something that a man or woman alone will not!

You can hold auditions in one of two ways:

- open – where auditions take place in front of all the other actors
- closed – where auditions are held in a separate room while the other actors wait to be called in another area.

The best way to organize the auditions is to block together the actors who are competing for the same character, so you can watch and compare them in sequence. If you are doing this, make sure the same person reads the other character in the audition piece each time, so it is a level playing field.

Then, of course, you will want to see the best of those actors for the respective parts play opposite each other to see how they look and work together. This process may necessitate at least one further audition session and, if you're undecided or unsure, by all means call the actors back for a third or even fourth audition.

Casting

Remember, you are casting the play by audition through your own understanding of the characters, but be open to the possibility that a performance from a particular actor may bring something else to the part. Casting is not solely about picking the best people. Factors such as how actors look, sound and work together, and the age of the overall cast, all come into play.

Actress A may be brilliant in the auditions as Juliet in *Romeo and Juliet*, but the fact that she is and looks 29 and is visibly pregnant would not make her a good casting choice for Juliet (an innocent youth, remember). Actor B may be great as the romantic lead, but since he is 6ft 5ins and his romantic opposite is 4ft 2ins that is visually not a good combination (unless deliberately comic), so you would have to revise the pairing.

During auditions you must recognize and take into consideration that the actors before you will invariably be nervous. There are some who do not read well but could be excellent actors, and there are others who do read well but do not act well – in both cases, listen to those people who know them within the drama group. You do not necessarily summarily dismiss these potential actors from your plans, but consider whether you could accommodate them elsewhere so that they may improve.

Director's rule No 3

Be wary of the actor who does not give their all in the audition, and try to recognize the potential of the nervous actor who might come on leaps and bounds on stage.

Once you have decided on your cast, contact all those who auditioned and tell them the good or bad news. Some actors will get the role they coveted and others, who you may feel are better suited to another part, will be offered an alternative role. Occasionally actors may turn down the role they are offered, so it is prudent to have a second or third choice for each role. It is wise, therefore, to do all the good news phone calls first.

When making the bad news phone calls to the unlucky band that has not been cast, always be polite and encouraging to the disappointed actors. Reassure them that you – and no doubt other directors in the drama group – would consider them for a role in future productions. Encourage them still to be part of the production, albeit in a non-acting capacity – for there is much to do.

Understudies

Choosing understudies is a decision that has to be seriously considered. Most community theatre productions run for a week and as such the appointment of understudies may not be worthwhile. Remember, additional rehearsal time will have to be given to the understudies and then there is also the issue of additional costumes.

Understudies may be actors playing minor characters from within the existing cast or actors who solely learn the part they are understudying. Time is an issue, but certainly for longer runs understudies are a wise investment, plus there is the advantage of seeing how another actor in the drama group copes with a major role.

Rehearsals

Schedule

Once you have cast the play you will have to draw up a rehearsal schedule, which can be a nightmare. Looking at the forms your actors filled in, you will have to accommodate any advised absences. This could mean rehearsing the play out of sequence. This is not really a disaster but a situation borne out of necessity. It can occasionally be a problem if you have an ensemble play where all the characters are required for every rehearsal. In this situation, an actor's availability (or lack of) could be an influencing factor in casting.

Absences and discipline

While you may plan for the advised absences of actors, the real disruption to rehearsals can be from non-advised absences. Usually there is a genuine reason why unscheduled enforced absences take place, such as family emergencies or being unavoidably detained in traffic. Both the director and the remaining cast have to take it on the chin and ask someone to stand in and read from the script. The problem with these absences is that they do not help the absent actor and are on occasion, through no fault of actor reading in, unhelpful to the cast that is present.

Sometimes there will be no satisfactory explanation as to why an actor is absent from rehearsals. If this a frequent occurrence then you should set up a mechanism by which the offending actor is removed from the cast and replaced with another more reliable actor. The circumstances for such a change need to be clearly established and supported by the committee in advance of rehearsals and made clear to the cast. As a director you need unequivocal support from the committee if such action has to be taken during rehearsals.

Additional rehearsals may be required to accommodate the new member of the cast to get up to speed. It is hoped that this type of situation will arise only rarely, if ever.

Read through

The next stage is to bring the cast and crew together for a formal read-through and general discussion about the play. The read-through can be an odd experience for the director because there will be actors who will read in the manner they intend to play the character while other actors may just read the words, still finding their way into the character.

It is also a session when a model of the set can be revealed and measurements of actors are taken for costumes.

Blocking

The first thing you will work on in rehearsal is blocking. Blocking is, in effect, bringing the physicality to the drama within the design of the set. It is the initial piece of directing for the actors' moves. Every move an actor makes must be motivated by the character and help tell the story. With that, the moves should focus the audience on the key action and enable them to follow the story.

Blocking is merely a starting point, however, and each move should be kept open for as long possible, until you are convinced it is the right one, at which point it should be committed to stone.

Experimentation

Rehearsals are about experimentation and seeing what works, but the important thing to remember is where you want the audience to be focused. Is it on the actor who is speaking (which is usually the case)? Is it on the actors listening and reacting to another actor's words? Both things should be happening in the scene, but as a director you decide what is important and where you want the audience's attention to be focused.

Movement should not take place unless it is necessary. Avoid placing actors too close together (unless the characters are being intimate). Sightlines are very important. An actor's face is expressive, so make sure the audience can see it.

Directing don'ts

There are certain moves on stage you should avoid instructing your actors to undertake, simply because it is poor stagecraft. So, don't:

- allow any actor to upstage any other actor. If you want a character to sit upstage, make sure they stay there until they become the main focus
- allow an actor to walk across the front of the stage in front of another speaking and/or sitting character
- allow actors to cross the stage in opposite directions (unless it is intentional)
- allow your actors to stand in a line (unless it is consciously intentional e.g. soldiers at attention)
- allow an actor to turn outward to exit if he/she is not the focus at that moment
- allow actors to move across the stage together, with one moving slightly later than the other.

However, since this is theatre, an artistic medium, there will always been exceptions and on that rare occasion when you may wish to do one or more of the above for a deliberate effect, it will become a *do* rather than a *don't*!

Look and listen

Although it may seem obvious, it is worth making the point that in rehearsals it is important to watch and listen to the action in front of you. The director should never have their face buried in the script or become distracted. They should make notes but should also be attentive.

The director has to be equally attentive to the actors and their comments and suggestions, and be prepared to try out others' ideas. Never be dismissive of an idea – the last thing you want is to curtail the creativity of a creative project – but if you turn down an idea, always explain why.

Scripts down

One significant date to include in your rehearsal schedule is when you expect your actors to have learned their lines, so that they can now rehearse without the aid of their scripts in their hands (certainly no later than four weeks before the performance). This is a significant transition period in the rehearsal process and does not pass by without a hiccup. It is now that you should have a prompter in the room – the person, ideally, who will act as prompt during the run, so they can recognize the actors' speech rhythms when they are saying their lines and not jump in with a prompt unnecessarily.

Run through

With the scripts out of the actors' hands, you will now be able to put the play together by beginning to run whole sections, scenes and complete acts. As the rehearsals progress, you will eventually reach the stage at which you will be able to run the whole of the play. You will still be open to amending as you see fit, both encouraging and correcting the actors through giving notes.

Giving notes

Throughout the rehearsal process, but more so in the latter stages, you will give notes. During each rehearsal you should be noting down the good, the bad and the problems of what you see before you. You should then convey those notes to the cast and crew accordingly. The fact is, you won't have much time to do this and so you must be direct and clear in what you say to the actors either individually or collectively. Be positive and make sure the actor has understood what you have said and what you are asking of them. If they don't understand, move on and then talk to them individually later.

When giving notes, do not lose your temper and never belittle any individual. There may be many reasons why an actor is not at their best on that particular rehearsal night – remember, you ultimately want them at their best on performance night – so you do not want to say or do anything that will affect their confidence.

Extra rehearsals

It is worth building into your rehearsal schedule additional dates where extra rehearsals may be utilized. This could be because some section just isn't working for one reason or another, but often it is because the actors request it themselves. Actors will always doubt themselves and their abilities and extra rehearsals are usually welcome and helpful. However, you must judge whether the extra rehearsals are actually needed because you do not want your cast overworked and peaking too soon before performance.

Technical rehearsal

The technical rehearsal ('the tech') is a very long day and will probably be the first time you see the set in a theatrical context. You will see if it looks as it should and works as it should with the doors, windows etc. If there are problems, a bit of last-minute DIY and set dressing may be required.

The tech will also be the time you will see if the lighting plot you have worked on with your lighting designer works. If it doesn't work, then you have to decide whether to change things on the lighting rig or the positioning of the actors.

You will hear whether the sound effects and music your sound designer has provided (usually on a laptop computer) actually work effectively in the theatre.

Be strong enough to say no and explore achievable alternatives with the designers and technicians in the time remaining. There may be financial implications for overruns at a theatre, which have to be considered.

At the tech you will get your actors to walk through all their entrances and exits, including timings for quick changes and any lighting and sound cues. It is not fun and at the end of it you will probably see your stage manager coming toward you with a list of glitches you will have to iron out before the next night's dress rehearsal, but you'll be pleased you found out about them at this stage rather than during a performance.

Dress rehearsal

The dress rehearsal will be the first and only time you will see the whole play performed before it goes before a paying audience the following night. Have your notebook on hand and give notes as you would for any other rehearsal, with the overriding message, irrespective of what happens, being a positive one.

The performance and afterwards

In theory you should be able to sit back and enjoy the performances that you have worked so hard to bring to the stage. Your trusted stage manager is in control and running the show, and the audience is filling the auditorium. In reality, you still have to watch and take notes and, like a football coach, go and gee up your team at the interval.

Interval

During the interval, make the effort to go backstage and give everyone an encouraging word about their performance and the positive reaction of the audience. You can do exactly the same at the end of a play while the warm glow of appreciative applause is still being felt.

Dealing with reviews

Newspaper reviews of the production are another aspect of the director's remit. A positive review can boost the cast and crew. Pin it up in the dressing room and let them read it and revel in its praise. However, sometimes there may be a negative review. The attitude to take is that the reviewer is only one person who did not reflect the view of the paying audience who went away happy. There may be a negative comment about a particular actor and you might have to lift the actor's spirits by concentrating on the positives of their performance and that fact that the reviewer didn't know what they were talking about!

Assistant director

If you have any desire to direct plays in the future, then the role of assistant director is a must. It is a rather ill-defined role in theatre, lacking the power of a stage manager or any clear responsibilities. However, in the role you will have the chance to see all aspects of being a director. The director may invite your views and ideas (be prepared to have them shot down) on the production and may also vent their anger and frustration on you when Ellie still can't remember her lines with only a week to go!

Playwright and director Alan Ayckbourn once told me of a director who used an assistant director to talk to the actors because he refused to speak to them! As an assistant director, if you encounter such a director, run away!

04

the stage manager

In this chapter you will learn:
- what a stage manager is
- what a stage manager does
- how to become a stage manager

What is a stage manager?

The stage manager (SM) is the trusted lieutenant of the community theatre world. In any production, the stage manager is a key appointment who can take a great deal of pressure and responsibility from the director. A good stage manager has the following qualities:

- good organizational skills
- diligent record keeping
- problem solver
- good humoured
- respected
- reasonable
- helpful
- honest
- communicative
- willing to take the initiative
- authoritative.

The stage manager is the director's most trusted aide and the person responsible for making the director's vision happen. The stage manager will work closely with all the various heads of department arranging frequent update meetings, organizing set and prop making and being on hand to solve any problems that may arise.

During rehearsals, they will be responsible for 'the bible' or 'the Book' – the copy of the script in which every cue for actors, lighting, sounds, props and set is recorded and described. It is from these notes in the SM's bible that a smooth production will emanate. Anyone with any problem needs to go to the SM for it to be resolved. Stage managers need to be aware of everyone and everything from get-in until get-out.

In addition, the SM can act as prompt – that is, supplying the actors with their lines if they forget them during a performance. Some of the responsibilities may be delegated to assistant stage managers, but still the stage manager needs to be kept informed at all times.

The stage manager will be in attendance throughout the rehearsal process and, if appointed early enough, will be part of the casting process alongside the director.

The stage manager will liaise and co-ordinate with the various departments of the creative team – set, costume, props, lighting, sound and publicity. They have the dual job of keeping the director informed of all things creative and arranging appropriate meetings between the creative team and the director.

If any problems arise, the initial reaction for the stage manager is to seek a solution within the parameters of the director's artistic brief. The SM will keep the director and the creative team informed of all events and thinking on the project.

The stage manager will sit alongside the director throughout the casting, auditioning and rehearsal process. Although the director may seek out their opinion on actors in auditions and casting, it is during rehearsals that good SMs can really show their worth.

Rehearsals

The stage manager will arrive early at rehearsals and, using tape, will mark out the dimensions of the acting area in the rehearsal room, including markings for entrances, exits and furniture, and placement of substitute furniture if the actual items are not available.

Throughout the rehearsal the SM will make notes in the Book.

The Book (bible)

The Book, or production bible, is the stage manager's copy of the script, in which the SM will create a definitive record of all staging decisions, including:

- every cut
- every textual change
- every move
- every stage direction
- every lighting cue
- every sound cue
- all other technical information.

Like an actor, the SM will have a pencil and eraser to record or amend these decisions.

The Book is the most precious production resource because the SM invariably can tell exactly where an actor was standing at any given time in a previous rehearsal, or what important gesture the actor performed that had an effect on the action which is not being repeated on this occasion.

At the end of, or even during, each rehearsal, the SM should be able to pass on, in a mini-report to the director, any potential problems they have picked up that the director may have missed.

The Book becomes invaluable as the production moves into the theatre because it will be used to 'call the show', cueing light, sound and special effects. All the notes in the Book should be clear so that, in theory, if anything happens to the SM, someone else should be able to understand and follow all the instructions written in its pages.

From the get-in, the stage manager becomes the boss of the production. They will ultimately be responsible for making the play happen as the director envisaged it.

Get-in

The stage manager will oversee the get-in, which is when the theatre group takes over the theatre, erecting and dressing the set, bringing in costumes and props and the setting up the technical aspects of the show. All these things are done by the relevant teams, but the SM is there to help and to deal with any problems that may arise.

Technical rehearsal

The stage manager will make sure all the cast and crew have signed into the theatre for the tech. Throughout the day, they will co-ordinate with the lighting and sound technicians to make sure the requested effects are as planned, and will then call the actors when it is time to do their walk through. They will be the point of call for anyone who has encountered any problems. The SM will then set about trying to iron these out in time for the dress rehearsal.

Dress rehearsal

During the dress rehearsal, the stage manager will run the show as a performance, from the signing in of cast and crew, calling the show, to dealing with unforeseen problems or accidents that arise from the run through.

On the night

On the night, the stage manager is responsible for:

- registering the cast and crew
- checking lighting, sound, special effects
- dealing with any pre-show problems
- calling the show.

Signing in

The stage manager needs to produce a list of all the cast and crew who are involved with the production. A list needs to be produced for each night from the technical rehearsal through to the final night. When any member of the production arrives at the theatre they must sign in on the appropriate list. The best practice is to delegate a member of the team – one of the ASMs – to be stationed at the stage door to catch people as they enter the theatre. Make sure each individual signs their signature against their own name. Do not allow anyone to sign in any other member of the cast or crew as this can cause confusion and uncertainty.

Once all the names have been signed, the ASM should inform the SM immediately that everybody is present. If anyone is late, the SM or ASM should contact the late arrival immediately to determine the situation. This may necessitate the SM having to decide whether to delay curtain-up or whether an understudy or stand-in needs to be enlisted for the impending performance. Similarly, if any backstage member is delayed the SM will need to arrange for their duties to be covered by the existing crew, or another member of the drama group needs to be called upon.

Checking lighting, sound and special effects

Working with the lighting and sound technicians in the theatre, the SM needs to check that everything technical is working and as it should be before the show begins. This should be done at the earliest opportunity and if any glitches are identified the SM should establish whether they can be ironed out before curtain-up. If not, the SM must contact the actors affected, inform them of the situation and present them with an alternative solution.

Calling the show

To 'call the show' the stage manager will usually sit in front of a monitor that relays a live feed of what is happening on stage. The SM will wear headphones and a mouthpiece and call from the Book all the lighting, sound and special effects cues to the linked technicians, who will instigate the instructions on command. The SM, following the script, will have established when they need to call the cue – or cues, as several may need to be called at the same time – taking into consideration the delay between instruction and actions. Most stage managers learn this instinctively and it leads to a seamless show. When effects are out of kilter, the audience will know it. The fact is that technicians will only act if you tell them to. They are practical people who look to the SM to guide them through the night. Occasionally, a technician will press the wrong button. Although this is not the SM's fault, they will have a word with the relevant technician at the end of the night to make sure it doesn't happen again.

Get-out

Once the final performance is finished, the SM will second as many people as possible from the cast and crew to help with the dismantling and removal of the set from the stage. It is important that this is done as quickly as possible as there may be financial penalties for the theatre group if they are not out of the theatre before the stated time in the contract.

How do I become a stage manager?

The best route is to serve as one of the assistant stage managers (ASM) on a production. You will learn about the different aspects and responsibilities associated with the SM's job and, as an ASM, you will certainly carry out some of the duties. Again, attend as many rehearsals as you can and help out where possible with the other aspects of production, such as costume and props. Talk to the people involved with the various departments and discuss the problems they face. Understand them and work with them because, as SM, you will have to coordinate them all.

How do I become an assistant stage manager?

The stage manager may enlist, indeed welcome, an assistant stage manager (ASM) to help with the burden of their role. There is no limit on the number of ASMs and they can be of enormous help from dealing and helping out with a specific department to acting as prompt. All the experience you get in this role will help you become a stage manager.

05

the lighting designer/technician

In this chapter you will learn:
- what the lighting designer/technician does
- how you become a lighting designer/technician
- the dos and don'ts of theatre lighting.

What is a lighting designer?

There are two aspects to theatre lighting, namely, designing and engineering. In community theatre both aspects are often merged and undertaken by one technician. We shall look at both aspects in this chapter.

The lighting designer (LD) must read the play, see the play and have a clear idea of the director's vision. In community theatre lighting designers do have a tough job. They usually have one day, if they're lucky, to set the lights in a theatre to see if the effect works as planned to the director's satisfaction.

If you're interested in lighting then the best thing to do is to get yourself a mentor within the society or local theatre or go on a course. NODA runs a summer school that offers such technical tuition. Many Little Guild Theatre members – that is, community theatre groups that own and run their own theatre – also offer workshops where you can get on-the-job training and have an on-site mentor. It is also worth checking with your local professional theatre to see if they host such workshops.

No group is ever going to allow you to step into the lighting designer/technician role unless they are convinced you know what you are doing. Lighting is not solely about sticking a spotlight on someone on stage. There are many types and shades of light and optical special effects and the lighting designer needs to be aware of the overall set and costume design, as well as basic concepts of whether a scene is staged at dawn, noon, afternoon, dusk or night or the general tone, intent, style and atmosphere of the play and the individual scenes. They have to be aware of shadows and blind spots and help direct the audience to the appropriate spot and action on the stage.

How to approach the role of lighting designer

Read the script and consult the director

At the earliest opportunity, the lighting designer needs to read the script and consult with the director, who should share their vision of the play. What is the tone of the play? Does the director have a particular lighting effect in mind? Will the play have few or many lighting changes? And if so, how does the director envisage those changes?

Talk to the creative backstage team

The LD should also consult with the set designer and costume department.

With regard to the set, look at the model the set designer should have produced. Look at the colour scheme, where every piece of furniture is and where there are doors or windows.

With regard to costume, again be aware of the colour, design and, importantly, the fabric being used. These can all have an effect on the lighting.

Research

Collect as many illustrations – usually photographs – as possible that show particular lighting techniques that can convey mood, style and effect. It helps to have a visual aide when discussing the lighting design with the director.

As a lighting designer you will have control over the type of light that shines on stage, giving due consideration to:

- intensity, e.g. the contrast on stage from dimness to blinding light
- colour e.g. not just of the lights but the costumes and other objects that are being illuminated
- distribution, e.g. definition of the light beam
- movement, e.g. from sunset to twilight to night in one scene.

Attend rehearsals

Everyone involved in the production of a play should at some point attend rehearsals, and that applies to lighting designers too. The movement of the actors can have an effect on the position and intensity of the lighting. In this respect, consult the stage manager and the production bible.

Designing the lighting

After all your consultations with fellow members of the creative team, you will be aware of what the lighting requirements are for the production. You should have an idea of the type of lighting effect needed and the position on the stage of the lighting. From this you will produce a rough lighting plot that will form the basis for the design of a lighting rig, indicating where and what type of lights and lanterns should be positioned on the rig, and indeed on and around the stage, and how they should be focused.

Lighting plot

Produce a scale drawing of the stage and set as seen from above and show, in detail, the lighting rig and where lights and lanterns should be fixed on it.

Vertical section plot

Produce a scale drawing of the stage and set seen in cross-section. This should show the vertical sightlines and the height and position of each piece of lighting equipment.

Instrument schedule

Each piece of lighting equipment should be listed, including details of its power and purpose, where it is plugged into and the appropriate command circuit (button or key) that activates it. This is important if any troubleshooting is required on the night. If you can quickly identify a lantern from switch to bulb you should be able to establish what the problem is and improve your chances of rectifying it quickly. It is also worth noting on the schedule back-up alternatives or replacements if a piece of lighting equipment should fail.

Cue sheet

Consultation with the stage manager and reference to the production bible is necessary for this. Make a complete list of all the lighting effects and their appropriate cues so that you fully understand what is required for the performance and in case there is a communications breakdown with the stage manager on the night.

Lighting dos and don'ts

Shadows – Be aware of where shadows may be cast by both immoveable and moveable objects on the set. Shadows conceal action from the audience and can be distracting; for example, an actor's moving shadow might be cast on stage as he waits in the wings.

Illuminate action – Theatre is a visual medium and the audience wants to see what is going on, so it is crucial that your lighting design clearly illuminates the action.

Light actors – Make sure all the actors on stage are lit unless the director has specified otherwise.

Under lighting – This is bad practice and, in effect, makes a scene too dark, concealing part of the set and the actors that need to be seen.

Over lighting – This is again bad practice because it can wash out the scene. The light is too bright and becomes difficult for the audience to watch.

Lighting design is an important art. Unfortunately, you will not know whether the design is practical and actually works until you are in the theatre. In effect, the design plot is rigged and tested on the day of the technical rehearsal.

Rehearsals

Plotting session

The plotting session is where the lighting design is rigged and then tested. In the initial test someone walks around the stage and takes up various positions to see the effect of the lights. Can the person be seen clearly? Does the beam need to be wider? Does the shadow from the wardrobe need to be countered with additional lighting? Does the beam reflect off the metal kettle?

Technical rehearsal

In the technical rehearsal the lighting designer will be able to see the actors move about on stage, primarily to get the lighting cues right but also, if they are in costume, to see what they look like under the lights. Costumed actors can change the look of the lighting. Look for shadows, particularly from characters wearing hats or over-elaborate hairstyles, and be aware of excessive reflection from items or clothing worn by the actors that could prove too distracting.

Dress rehearsal

The dress rehearsal will be the only time before performance when you will be able to see whether the lighting really does have the correct tone and conveys the right atmosphere. It is the only time you will be able to practise the lighting cues in real time. Does the cross-fade work? Is the blackout at the end of Act Two effective? And so on.

On the night

The lighting designer/technician needs to do a light check before the audience arrives. They need to know that all the lights and lanterns work, that the effect from the lighting is as it should be. If there is a problem it needs to be fixed, e.g. if a bulb has gone, it needs to be replaced.

When the curtain goes up the lighting technician will normally be sitting in front of a console called the lighting desk, in a room at the back of the auditorium. Through headphones they will be in contact with the stage manager, who will call the lighting cues. Once the stage manager has called the cue the lighting technician will implement this and all subsequent lighting cues throughout the night.

Problems

Lighting problems, namely, a light fails to work, usually come from a technological breakdown. Troubleshooting will involve checking the connection or the bulb or the software. The best policy, if possible and resources allow, is when designing a rig to have back-up alternative lighting in place that could do a similar job.

For any repair issue time is of the essence, particularly if it involves a technician climbing up on a lighting rig. Judgements have to be made as to whether it is practical to deal with the problem as the show goes on, wait for the interval or have it resolved ready for the following night.

06

the sound designer/technician

In this chapter you will learn:
- what the sound designer/technician does
- how to become a sound designer/technician
- the dos and don'ts of theatre sound.

'I always say, if you've got a hi-fi at home and you're used to controlling the volume and setting the tone that you like, you can run a sound desk. There just may be a few more knobs on there!'

David Green, Sound Designer/Engineer, Leicester Little Theatre and Leicester Drama Society

What is a sound designer?

The sound designer is responsible for sourcing an array of sound effects for a production. It can be anything from a howling storm on a heath for *King Lear,* the bleating of farm animals, to gun fire, doorbells, telephones, voice distort devices, music and much more.

Sound designers have the benefit, with the right equipment, of bringing some, if not all of their special effects and music into the rehearsal room. This gives the actors and director the chance to experience them and check that they work and are appropriate. With sound effects, the noises are there to enhance a scene and not overwhelm it, so actors' words must not be lost in a cacophony of sound.

For sound effects, technology is much more user friendly and accessible than it used to be. Effects can be sourced from SFX CDs or the internet, or can be created and recorded with inexpensive digital equipment. Most of the sounds are then burned on to a production CD ready to be cued and played in rehearsal and performance.

Work with the sound people in your society and learn more about the techniques and sources they use. Some theatres, both amateur-owned and professional, may run workshops and courses for would-be sound technicians and designers. Certainly many members of the Little Theatre Guild can offer a mentoring scheme to anyone interested in theatre sound and finally allow them to take charge of their own production.

For any production there may be a sound engineer/designer involved and, if you're interested, assist and learn from them on the next production.

How to approach the role of sound designer

The first thing the sound designer must do is read the script and make notes of where a sound effect should be heard and what its probable duration may be. For example, a distant gun shot is a one-off event but must be heard at a precise moment in the play. A sound with a longer duration could be the unseen crowd outside a balcony window, or an on-going air raid or music played on the radio.

From the script you should draw up a list of sound effects that are explicit or implicit in the text. Explicit will be sounds that the characters refer to or react to in dialogue. Implicit sounds may come from the setting, e.g. the sea if a scene is set on a beach; the trill of song birds in the garden if the scene is set in the spring.

Take your list and ideas to the arranged meeting with the director and stage manager.

Meeting with the director

The director may have specific ideas about the type of sound he/she wants from what you, as the sound designer, have listed. Any sustained piece of sound may have to undulate, becoming more prominent at certain times during the scene. A soundscape will have to be created. The director may want a particular piece of music playing on the radio (if it is not specified in the script).

Sourcing sound

Many generic sound effects – ranging from wild animals to intergalactic star battles – can be found on CD or on certain internet sites. These sound effects are invariably copyright-free and can be readily used by community theatre groups. However, these generic sound effects may not be appropriate – they may not sound right or be too short or indistinct. This may lead you to create your own sound effects.

On occasion, the real sound of a given object may not sound as it should when recorded. When this happens you may have to manufacture a recording by doing something that produces the kind of sound you want. This will require experimentation and patience until the right sound is recorded.

The sound designer/engineer needs to understand that any sound created on their laptop is going to be amplified in the theatre, and volume can affect not only the quality but the nature of the sound. Before you get into the theatre, test the sound through the biggest speakers you can find.

Sourcing music

When sourcing recorded music for the production, the designer will have to remind the production team that any additional music used in the play may require a PRS (Performing Rights Society) and/or PPL (Phonographic Performance Limited) licence to be used.

It terms of sound, it will need to be determined if the music is to be realistic or theatrical. Is it merely background music from the radio or used to counter-point the action?

Underscoring

The director may want music to underscore the dialogue on stage. The sound designer needs to consider the balance between words and music. Finding the right music and playing it during rehearsals is the only way to establish whether the music is right for the scene and gain an indication of what level the music should be at in the theatre when the play is being performed.

Bridging music

The director may feel music is required to bridge the gap between scenes when changes to the set are being made. In this regard, the music needs to be in keeping with the play: if it is a comedy, happy, upbeat music should be used; if the genre edges towards horror, a more sombre or uncomfortable style of music would be required. The bridging music may be used to show a change of mood, but it has to be carefully selected. Bridging music is played briefly, depending on the swiftness of the scene change, and is often faded in and faded out again. A good tip is to find the main musical theme or chorus of the music or song and use that part of the recording for the bridging music.

Microphones

Generally speaking, most plays and comedies do not require the use of microphones. The actors' voices should be strong enough to carry the dialogue. However, there may be plays where an actor's voice needs to be distorted, perhaps because he/she is playing an android. In this case, source the microphone that can produce the voice distortion you require. What has to be borne in mind is that since the actor's voice is boosted with a microphone, the voice will still need to be balanced with the normal projected voices of the rest of the cast. If possible, test this in rehearsal.

Sound master

Once all the sounds and music have been sourced and approved, they need to be catalogued and a running order established before transferring them to whatever piece of computerized equipment you will be using to play the sound effects to the audience in the theatre. There are now numerous options, such as laptops, digital samplers, CDs, CD-ROMs, laser disc, mini disc or whatever the latest technology is (do keep up to date), plus the good old-fashioned sound desk, but all do the same job.

Sound properties

The sound designer/engineer can control five elements of sound in the theatre. These are:

- volume – the loudness of the sound
- pitch – the level or tone of the sound
- quality – the combination of volume and pitch
- direction – the movement of sound in relation to audience and/or cast
- duration – the length of time the sound lasts.

Designing the sound

Sound plot

The sound designer/engineer, after consulting with the stage manager, referring to the production bible and attending rehearsals, should draw up a sound plot, that is, a complete list of all music and sound effects along with cues of when they start and finish. Although almost everything can now be placed on a single CD, this may not be the case and so the plot should indicate from which piece of equipment the sound is to be played and through which speakers it is to be conveyed to the audience. Even if everything is on CD, each sound effect must have its track number listed and a back-up CD should be made available in case anything happens to the first.

System layout

The sound designer should produce a drawing that shows the type and position of all the speakers on the stage. It is also wise to indicate from where the power is sourced and where the connection wires are, just in case a problem occurs and has to be solved as quickly as possible, particularly on the night.

Cue sheet

A cue sheet for all sound and music needs to be drawn up for reference during the performance, listing when a sound should be played, its duration, volume and fade in/out details.

Rehearsals

Technical rehearsal

The 'tech' will be the first time the sounds you've sourced and recorded will be played in the theatre. During the technical rehearsal you will establish or confirm the levels and playing times of each track.

Dress rehearsal

The dress rehearsal will be the first time the effects and music of the soundtrack will be played in the context of the whole production. By the end of this you will have a definitive soundscape of tone and volume for the rest of the performance week.

On the night

On arrival at the theatre, do check that all the sound effects and music are there and working, and always have a back-up version to hand just in case the soundtrack has been damaged or corrupted in anyway. Like your lighting colleague, you will be in direct contact with the stage manager who will call the sound cues for you to instigate. All you need to know are the controls for on, off, fade in, fade out and volume.

Note: Also refer to the Chapter 10 for the different demands of sound design in musical theatre.

07

the set designer

In this chapter you will learn:
- **what the set designer does**
- **the dos and don'ts of set design**
- **the considerations of set building.**

What is a set designer?

A set designer is the person responsible for the look and practicality of the set – the world which the characters of the play inhabit. Set designers tend to be artistic and visually orientated, and yet they must have a down-to-earth practicality. What they design has to work for the actors on stage and the watching audience.

The best set designers usually have had some training but, like anything else in theatre, you can learn the basic tenets of set design by undertaking workshops and courses at theatres, schools and colleges.

How to design a stage set

Read the play

The first step to designing a stage set is to get hold of a copy of the play and read it. Take note of where the play is set. Is it inside or outside? Is it all set in one room? What is the room? Is it a lounge? Is it a bedroom? Is it an office? Is it a forest? Are there scene changes?

Take note of when it is set. Is it the 1960s? Is it in classical Rome? Is it contemporary?

Take note of the situations within the play. Is there a dinner? Is there a dance? Is there a fight? Is there a seduction? Does the house fall down?

The director's interpretation and vision

You will have a meeting with the director at an early stage to establish what their personal vision for the play is. The director may want to update the play and bring it forward to a new time period. They may want it to be classical or gritty or pantomime in tone. Also establish whether the director wants to include any strong visual images – he/she may want a character to come up through a trap door in Act Three, so you don't want to put a sofa in that position.

Any ideas you have about the set should be given at the meeting and, in all the likelihood, the director will give them due consideration.

Research

If you're dealing with a specific time period it is worth researching the interior design and fashion of that year. Wallpaper, furniture and white goods design can all convey a time period that is recognisable to the audience and is worth a thousand words of exposition by a character about when and where they are! Based on this research you can think about the design, but remember, you are not making a documentary – your stage set just needs to convey the time period.

The basic needs of the play

Getting the actors on and off stage is one of the practicalities of theatre and so, as a set designer, you have to consider how many entrances/exits there are and where they should be positioned.

Is there a staircase? Are there windows? Is there more than one location?

Other considerations may include the positioning of the furniture. The maxim of any set design is to keep it simple. No stage set should be cluttered and nothing should be on the set if it does not serve a purpose.

What action takes place?

One of the reasons stage sets need to be simple is that the focus will and should always be on the actors. If a stage set is cluttered it may be difficult, for example, to choreograph a stage fight between two actors. Think about the maximum number of actors who may be on stage at any one time. They will all need space.

Is a landline telephone important to the action? How often is it used? Where should it be positioned? Do characters have to hide from view? Is a painting on the wall important? If it is, should it be central?

The set will evolve from conversations between the set designer and the director about the latter's vision and interpretation of the play. The set designer needs to read the play and understand the practicalities relating to the action, such as the number of exits, types of door and how everything is treated. Does action switch from the drawing room to the bedroom?

Models and blueprints

It is essential to create small-scale physical representations of the set before the real thing is built. The blueprints for the builders will be based on these.

Set model 1

Once you have a clear view of what is needed, make a white scale model of the stage set, including all the pieces of furniture correctly positioned. You will need to look at the model stage at eye level and consider audience sightlines and whether the proportions are correct.

After showing the model to the director, do a second version of the set model, incorporating any feedback the director may have given.

Set model 2

The second set model should be a coloured and textured version. This will involve some experimentation because you may find that the colours and décor you envisaged do not work visually. Once you are satisfied, go back to the director. The director will react in one of three ways:

- accept the design and give the go-ahead for construction
- largely accept the design but suggest one or two amendments
- reject the design.

If you get the go-ahead for your design from the director, move on to the set-building phase. If the director suggests amendments, make these and have the revised model approved.

If the design is rejected, find out exactly why the director does not like it. It may be that they don't like the whole thing or you may only need to amend a few things. If the director truly does not like the design, sit down with them and establish exactly what they want. Some directors like to think set designers possess ESP, but they don't, they need to be given clear guidance.

Blueprints

Set designers must be prepared for the director to reject their ideas at the model stage for any number of reasons, but once the okay is given, the set designer will need to draw up – and the word cannot be emphasized enough – *precise* blueprint drawings for the set builders. From the outset, the specifications of the theatre stage and wings (where a bedroom, for example, may be stored until it's needed) needs to be known – it is within this space that the set will be built. The set designer will know these details from their scale models.

Set construction/builders

Set building is a practical pastime that can include sawing, screwing, nailing, painting, testing etc. Consideration has to be given to assembling, dismantling and transportation of the set. Set builders need to be very much aware of the practicalities of what they are making and what it does. Does it need to move? Is it stable when all 14 members of the cast stand on it?

Scenery is a façade and, largely speaking, only needs to look good on one side. It has to be sturdy and yet flexible. Stage sets, it has to be remembered, are not made to last but are temporary and reusable in another guise.

> 'We had a young man in our group, and I remember one time I wanted a farmhouse kitchen end that would move on wheels and wheel off. By the time he finished it you couldn't move it. You couldn't get it off stage because we were restricted in space and we ended up pushing it to one side of the stage and covering it with other scenery to disguise it because, in his world, if he built something he'd build it to last. Stage scenery isn't built to last to time immemorial!'
>
> *Mina Kirkbright of St Phillip's Amateur Dramatic Society*

Once everything has been made to specifications (or borrowed), the set will need to be painted and dressed. It has to be remembered that the set will always be seen from a distance and what people can see on the front row should be recognisable to people on the back row.

In the theatre

The set is not seen in its full glory until the get-in, when the set is constructed and dressed. The set designer, along with the stage manager, will see that it is assembled properly and everything is in its right place. All moving parts, such as doors and windows, need to be checked to see if they work properly.

Technical rehearsal

It is important to check that everything looks the way it should under the stage lights. The technical rehearsal will be the first time the set is seen under lights, so take a walk around the auditorium to check all the sightlines as this should uncover any faults. It may reveal unforeseen problems that necessitate moving part of the set because of the shadows, or changing an aspect or angle of the set due to an eye-catching reflection for the audience. If something needs concealing or buffing up with paint, polish or an extra cushion, do it!

If scene changes are required where scenery is taken on and off stage, this will be tried out and rehearsed with the backstage crew until it is quick and smooth.

Dress rehearsal

The set designers and their team won't see the full effect of their work until the dress rehearsal, when the whole play is run as a performance with actors in costume, lighting changes and sound effects. It is perhaps only then that you can be sure that the whole concept has worked and that the scene changes are slick and safe for cast, crew and audience alike. If the concept hasn't worked all you can do is make the best of it – and learn for next time.

08

wardrobe

In this chapter you will learn:
- what the costume designer does
- what the wardrobe team does
- what factors to consider in costume design.

The wardrobe team

The wardrobe department will be led by a costume designer and assisted by a creative team. The costume designer not only originates the look but is on hand until the end of the production ready to make instant repairs.

The timetable for the wardrobe team is as follows:

- measurements of cast
- manufacture or sourcing of costumes
- actors trying on costumes – with subsequent adjustments
- costume plot
- dress rehearsal
- performances.

The costume designer

The costume designer is responsible for the look of the characters in the play, which is guided by the director's vision in conjunction with the set design and lighting design. The costume designer should be talking to (and vice-versa) the designers of set, lighting and props to get an overall feel of the production. The budget always dictates what costume designers can or can't do. They have to be aware of their resources with regard to who will make the new clothes once the designs have been approved. Good costume designers are fantastically creative people who adhere to the mantra of community theatre, 'beg, steal or borrow', to get the best look from the resources available.

Costume designers have to placate the actor who is convinced he has a 36-inch waist, when in reality it is 40 inches! They have to consider what looks good but is also practical for the art of acting. A good costume team is vital to any production. They work very hard and don't sign off until the last night's curtain call. They will be on hand to quickly fix that lost button or ripped strap.

The script

Costume designers must be familiar with the script and be aware of the overall design of the production. Is the play set in a particular period and/or place? Reference to history books is a must for any self-respecting costume designer. Designers have an eye for detail that may seem irrelevant to the actor but which adds an authenticity to the production. That eye for detail extends to hairstyles and make-up, which form the overall look of the character.

Indeed, clothes are a reflection of a character's status, relationship and attitude. When you go shopping for clothing you tend to pick clothes that you think look good on you and reflect your personality. It is exactly the same for characters in a stage play.

There are practical issues to address regarding costumes too. The script will offer an insight into the potential wear and tear of a costume, so potential problems can be anticipated, accommodated and eradicated. When reading the script, the wardrobe team should identify what is being asked of the characters and the actors who portray them.

- Does the script reveal absolute necessities for the costume?
- Are there hidden pockets?
- Does a gun or knife need to be safely concealed?
- Does anyone get covered in blood or custard pies?
- Will the fabric wash easily and be good as new and unblemished for the next night's performance?
- Do characters have to fight or dance?
- Does anyone have a quick costume change? Velcro is good and buttons are a pain in the neck.
- Does anyone have to get dressed and/or undressed on stage?

Acquiring costumes

Making costumes

The wardrobe department of any community theatre group is constrained by resources and budget. Designing costumes for a whole range of characters is a time-consuming but creative role. Designers have to combine consistency with the necessities of the characters and the practicalities of the world the characters inhabit.

An additional challenge comes when converting the design patterns into actual costumes to be worn by actors. First, the material has to be sourced on a beg, steal or borrow basis. Once that is achieved, you need a team who know how to cut and sew and are able to make adjustments, embellish and produce wonderful costumes on an extremely limited budget – and they invariably do.

If they are subsequently looked after and stored correctly, those newly designed and handmade costumes, particularly for popular shows, can become an asset and a source of extra income for the group as they can be hired out to other societies.

Sourcing costumes

Of course, not all costumes are made from scratch (or thin air, a costume designer once told me) – sometimes they can be hired. The wardrobe team will be responsible for sourcing these. This is useful for musical productions since, in reality, there are not that many musicals and there is almost a standard look to shows like the *King and I* or any Gilbert & Sullivan musical. However, hiring costumes is an expensive business and, as such, budgetary considerations dictate that the costumes can arrive as late as the dress rehearsal and may then require alterations. (Bear in mind that the contract with the hiring firm may forbid you from significant alterations, so check before undertaking any changes to hired costumes.) There is also the danger of not receiving all of the requisite costumes on time.

Depending on the type of play being performed, costumes may be sourced from charity shops, from chain stores with unwanted stock or from the actors' own wardrobes. You may also contact other drama groups and hire from them, or see if a sponsor will donate a range of appropriate costumes and clothing for your latest production.

Accessories

Clothing accessories such as gloves, hats, jewellery and watches are as important to the look of the character as the main costume. It is these accessories that can make a particular character distinctive to the audience.

Costume plot

The costume designer will have to create a costume plot. This document should list when characters appear, what they are wearing (costume and accessories) and if they need a costume change (quick or otherwise). It is prudent to delegate members of the wardrobe team to help actors undertake costume changes for each performance, particularly quick costume changes. The plot should include when and where actors enter and exit so that an appropriate member of the wardrobe team is stationed at the right place at the appropriate time.

On the night

On the night, the wardrobe team will be represented backstage to do one of two things:

- help with an actor's quick costume change, or
- help with maintenance and repair to any actor's costume during the performance.

At the end of the run it is important for the wardrobe team to collect and account for every piece of costume (including accessories) from the actors. If the costumes are hired, there may be financial penalties for damaged or lost costumes.

The make-up artist

Most basic make-up can be self-applied by actors but anything more extensive requires the skills of a make-up artist.

If you are interested in theatrical make-up then do join a community theatre group as most have members who will encourage you and impart their knowledge about the subject. There are workshops and courses you can attend and some accessible books on the subject where you can learn about the different materials and what to consider when applying make-up such as face shape and skin type. You will learn how to achieve the best effect with the materials available and learn the practicality and skill of how quickly it can be applied and/or removed. Think of the actor who is healthy in one scene then injured or diseased in the next or vice versa.

Theatrical make-up is about experimentation and very much a doing activity. Practise on faces, particularly if you want to try something new or the director wants a particular look. Surprisingly, there will be a lot of actors quite happy to let you loose on their face. Theatrical make-up adds to the character they are portraying and they will be impressed at how you can transform them. So much so they quite possibly won't let anyone else 'do' their face – even the basic stuff!

During the rehearsal period do experiment until you get the look the director wants. Arrange sessions with the actor and, if the director cannot be present, take photographs. Once the look has been achieved you will need to time yourself to see how long the make-up process takes. Inform the stage manager and they will instruct the actor to be attendance on the night by a set time according to your needs.

On the night

The make-up artist will arrive early with all his/her appropriate materials. He/she, with their team, will then begin the process of applying the make-up to the characters. You will work to a rota, calling actors at a given time (or earlier) in the order you have worked out.

Throughout the performance there maybe minor touching-up of an actor's make-up or an actor may require a major make-over due to the events that befall his character. Most playwrights understand that the application of major make-up does take time and will either take the actor offstage just before the interval or offstage for a significant portion of the play before being returned to the limelight transformed. Nevertheless, speed and efficiency are of the essence for you and your team.

09

the props team

In this chapter you will learn:
- what props are
- what the props team does in pre-production
- what the props team does on the night.

What are props?

Properties, or props as they are more popularly known, are anything an actor could potentially utilize on stage. There are basically two types of props – personal and stage. Personal props are anything an actor will carry and use, such as a letter, a gun or a lighter. An alternative and more self-explanatory term for these items is hand props.

Stage props are any items to do with the set, such as furniture, telephones, lamps and so on. These will be dictated by the set designer, and it is likely that a member of the props team will be the set dresser.

The significant thing to remember about props is that if they have to be used or powered, make sure that they work and that the actors know how to work them. The actors have to be familiar with their environment because everything they do must seem natural rather than as if something has been handed to them just a week before. For example, if you ask an actor in a Georgian costume what the time is, their instinct is to look at their wrist as opposed to the pocket watch chained to their waistcoat!

The role of the props team

The job of the props team is to create and/or source the props to be used in the production. As always, the first task is to discover what props are actually needed, which can only be done by reading the script. The props supervisor will use the script to compile a list of the necessary props. Further props may be added to the list as actors develop their characters and rehearsals reveal further opportunities for these affectations.

The job of the props team requires resourcefulness and inventiveness when sourcing these items, either through purchasing or hiring the ready-made article, or making the prop. A degree of research is required, particularly if the play is a period piece, with due consideration of the set and costume design.

On the night

Personal props are the responsibility of the actor, but there have been many occasions on which a vital prop, such as revelatory letter or murder weapon, has gone astray. The prop's non-appearance in the crucial scene can undo a play. The best policy is, once the prop has been used it should be returned to a specific place on the props table, manned by a member of the props team, so it can be made available either later on or for another actor to use. If an actor does not return the prop to the table straight after they have come off stage then one of the props team must go and retrieve it, possibly giving the actor a good telling off.

One excellent props supervisor once told me that she reminded errant actors that it wasn't going to be her who would be publicly embarrassed under the stage lights, in front of an audience and in the subsequent newspaper review if the all-important prop did not appear on cue!

Like costumes, a prop may require ongoing maintenance, particularly if it has to endure regular battering throughout the play. At the beginning of the night it should look brand new and by the end no use to anyone. Several versions of one item may be required to reflect this. Then there is the possibility that a prop becomes damaged beyond repair. In this instance, the props team should anticipate the possibility in advance and judge whether a back-up copy or duplicate is required.

Scene shifters

Scene shifters are the people dressed in black who flit to and fro across stage to add or remove items from the set between scenes. This group of people are self-choreographed, doing their tasks as quickly as possible, removing and/or adding tables, chairs, props and scenery.

It has to be said that good backstage people are like gold dust and if you show an aptitude for or interest in any of those roles, any society will snap you up and cherish you. Find like-minded individuals who have no desire to act and you could form your own community theatre group based solely on backstage talent (see the case study on the next page).

Case study

The Penguin Club – Community Theatre group not for actors!

The Penguin Club is the Cambridge-based community theatre group that does not stage plays or musicals but specializes in supplying backstage talent to other groups and societies on a production-by-production basis.

'We were noticing that the same group of people were meeting to do the backstage work, people who weren't interested in acting or going out in front of the lights. So they got together one day and decided to work together and coordinate these things and formed what was to become the Penguin Club,' explained treasurer Alan Baker.

On 1 November 1983 the Penguin Club was formed and ever since they have been training and supplying backstage talent to a whole host of community theatre groups and musical societies in the Cambridge area. They have a 60-strong membership and, like other conventional groups, welcome new members.

'No qualifications are needed other than an interest and wanting to get involved. We have people who do lighting design and operation, set building, painting and sound, stage management etc. People who have no experience join us because they like the idea of it. We train them and see what they like to do and encourage them in one direction or another.

'We only serve the interests of what people want to do. We supply bodies and expertise, not equipment, although most people have their own tools.'

Training

'There are two ways to train: we do on-the-job training so, for example, if you fancy helping with lights, you'd go along and work with the lighting designer and electrician and learn as you go along, and pick it up. Depending on their ability some people pick it up and others don't.

'Occasionally, a couple times a year, we will try and run training days at a theatre or stage somewhere and show people what the lights are, show them how to fly and show them how to carry stuff properly and do the general backstage work. We turn up at a building where the stage has been built and show everyone how everything works.'

The Penguin Club supplies either individuals for particular roles or groups with the necessary backstage expertise, and the commitment to the theatre group or musical society can vary.

'Stage managers, lighting designers, set builders, etc. will get involved at a fairly early stage of a production. For example, some of our members were involved as set builders for a December production of *Beauty and the Beast* but they were involved from the beginning of September working on the set and were involved two months before in the production meetings. Other members doing other roles, of course, may only become involved at the get-in.'

Members of the Penguin Club are in constant demand, but no one member is ever under any pressure to do a show. The members can pick and choose the projects in which they are interested. A theatre group will approach the Penguin Club with a list of backstage personnel they need to fill. Members are consulted and the Penguin Club then informs the group of which positions they can fill for their production.

Of course, with a name like Penguin Club, people would not necessarily associate the group with theatre, let alone backstage talent.

'There are lots of stories about how we got the name, but the most reasonable is, obviously, that we dress in black and wander about in the dark, and when you're carrying heavy set you look like you're waddling. However, the first chairman liked penguins and had a collection of penguin ornaments and the like!'

You can visit the Penguin Club website at **www.penguinclub. org.uk.**

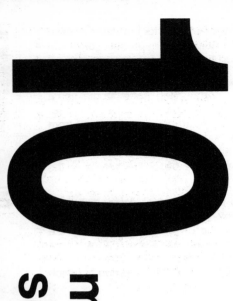

10

musical societies

In this chapter you will learn:
- how musicals differ from plays in applying for rights
- how musicals differ from plays in auditions, rehearsal and production
- about the different roles in musical societies.

Let us turn our attention now to operatic and musical societies for which there are different demands upon the newcomer and established performer. Before being accepted as a member of a musical society you will have to audition. For this audition you will be allowed to sing your own choice of song. The society will be looking at whether you can sing in tune and your ability to hold a harmony. They may also want an indication of your acting and/or dancing ability.

A musical society may stage the full gamut of musicals while others may specialize in the work of, for example, Gilbert & Sullivan. Determine what interests you and obviously apply accordingly. If you're accepted you will then be able to audition for the musicals staged by the society.

Staging a musical is an expensive business, and often musical societies engage professionals in key roles such as producer, musical director, choreographer and musicians. These roles may also be undertaken by the society's own amateur members.

Who's who

Producer

In musicals the producer, in effect, is the director. He/she is in overall charge of the production and it is their vision that is finally seen on stage. The role of producer in community theatre is sometimes allocated to a paid professional for whom a contract needs to be drawn up between the society and the producer concerned (you can get a model contract for directors/producers from NODA).

Normally, the producer is responsible for the casting of the musical. He/she will sit with the musical director and, if needed, choreographer and take expert advice about the actor's vocal and dance ability. There may also be independent society members sitting with the producer to pass any relevant information on to them before casting. The producer will then present their cast list to the committee for ratification.

However, on occasions the producer will have no control over the casting whatsoever. It may be that the professional is not a member and, although the producer may make recommendations, it will be the committee who cast the play.

This can mean the producer working with a cast they perceive as not the best available.

A professional producer may do the same show with several different societies over a given period. This is good, financially for the producer and potentially for the societies as they are engaging someone who is already familiar with the production. It can mean the producer makes small changes to their next production, taking into consideration the personnel, venue, etc. rather than starting from scratch. However, some producer's are rigid. Once they have done the show it is a blueprint set in stone, irrespective of the society with whom they are working. This does not necessarily lead to good theatre. It is worth researching the producer's previous work before engaging him/her on your production.

The producer will merge together the music, choreography and actors into a unified and, hopefully, seamless show. They have to know how to use the chorus effectively, bring out the best performance of the principal actors and direct the audience to the focal point of a scene on an often crowded stage.

Musical director

A musical director (MD) is responsible for all music-related aspects of the production. This role is usually for musicals and, quite frankly, you have to have a damn good working knowledge and experience of music. For this reason a fair percentage of musical societies engage a professional musical director. In this case there should always be a written contract between the society and the musical director concerned, which makes clear what is expected of the MD and, similarly, what the MD expects from the society. There is always a danger that an individual may walk away from the production and leave the society in the lurch and, without a written contract, the society has no comeback.

During casting, the producer of a musical will often be dependent on the musical director's recommendations regarding the vocal range and ability of the actors auditioning for the various roles. The musical director then works and rehearses with the main players on their songs, as well as working with the chorus. He/she will also be responsible, if the society doesn't have their own, for the sourcing and engaging of musicians, be it a single pianist, a four-piece rock band or a 32-piece orchestra. If professional musicians are engaged, again, a written contract needs to be drawn up. The musical director will be responsible for the musical arrangements and will work closely with the producer.

The MD will bring all the vocal and instrumental elements together into a cohesive unit and, on performance night, will be the conductor and be responsible for the smooth running of all things musical.

Choreographer

The choreographer works in close consultation with the producer and musical director, uniting the producer's vision with the musical director's musical work through dance. Again, this is a specialist role and the choreographer will need a proven knowledge of choreography and be very aware of the physical abilities of the dancing troupe.

Musicians

Community musical societies are likely to engage professional musicians for their productions, and if those musicians are members of the Musicians Union or the venue is subject to the MU and the Theatre Managers' Association Agreement, then there is a set contract and salary rates and other fees that apply. Unfortunately, engaging professional musicians is a significant expense and as a result the musicians don't get involved until very late in the production process and often will not meet with the rest of the cast until the technical/dress rehearsals. Sometimes an informal rehearsal with cast and musicians can take place before the technical rehearsal.

The financial concerns, of course, do not apply to amateur musicians. Their involvement can be as much or as little as they are willing to give. Amateur musicians have the advantage of being able to work with the musical director more on a given production.

However, since the musical director is often responsible for sourcing musicians he/she will inevitably go to familiar professional or amateur musicians with whom they have previously worked.

Choosing a musical

The first decision is to select a musical and make sure of its availability. This can be done by contacting the appropriate rights holders. Not all musicals will be available to be staged by amateur companies. A West End run or a national tour could restrict amateur rights availability to certain geographical areas or they simply may not be available at all. On occasions there may be a brief window of opportunity to stage a highly successful musical such as Willy Russell's *Blood Brothers* when amateur rights become available, so it is important to pay attention to what new musicals come on to the market, as it were. The various right holders will trumpet any new arrivals on their respective websites or through print advertising in publications such as *NODA News* or *Amateur Theatre*.

The works of Gilbert & Sullivan are out of copyright so the question of rights availability is no longer an issue. Specialist musical societies such as Gilbert & Sullivan have a limited canon to draw upon – a maximum of 13 operas – so they will probably choose the production they haven't staged for ten years or so. That formula can equally apply to other musical societies.

Licensing

The licensing procedure for musicals is different from plays. No licence fee is paid in advance, although you will have to pay a deposit, as usually the licence fee for musicals is calculated as a percentage of box-office takings. However, musical societies still need to apply for a performance licence and enter into agreement with the appropriate agents in advance. Written permission has to be received by the musical society before the production can go ahead. Once the production has finished, the musical society must send in details of their box-office returns. They will then be issued with an invoice for a percentage of those takings to pay the licence fee, which then has to be paid.

Josef Weinberger Limited

Josef Weinberger Limited has been involved in musical rights and publishing since 1885 and handles the amateur rights to a diverse range of musical plays ranging from Viennese operettas to modern 21st-century stage shows such as *The Witches of Eastwick* and *High School Musical*. They are also responsible for the Rodgers & Hammerstein musicals. Since 1998 they have also become involved in plays, taking over Warner Chappell Plays and the New York Dramatists catalogue.

'When an organization is planning to perform a musical or play, they must make contact with the relevant rights holder to check the availability. We would require the name of the organization, venue details and performance dates in order to see whether the show was available. At this stage we couldn't guarantee a licence until the relevant completed licence application forms have been returned to us and our requirements have been met.

'We suggest organizations apply for a licence as far in advance as possible in case the show or play they wished to perform becomes withdrawn for any reason. Plays and musicals are usually withdrawn if there is a professional production or tour being organized. We do as much as possible to negotiate with the touring companies to release rights in areas where their tour is not playing, however, this is not always possible. To break copyright law by performing without the appropriate licence is an offence and as agents/owners of our works, we have to protect the authors' interests by taking any relevant legal action.'

Ian Reeder, Licensing Department, Josef Weinberger Limited

Musicals are popular, but it is fair to say some musicals and G&S operas are more popular than others. Doing your homework on what your local audience likes and/or dislikes will be an important piece of research. Musicals are very expensive productions to stage because they require many performers on stage, musicians and a large backstage support group. Costs are high and so it is very important that a realistic budget is in place. Know what your costs are and what you are realistically going to take at the box office. Serious financial loss in a musical can lead to the folding of the company. We will assume at this point that a realistic budget has been put in place.

Auditions and casting

Pre-audition rehearsals

A common practice in amateur musical theatre is to run at least one pre-audition rehearsal. Some societies run more and the number can vary from production to production and from society to society. The idea is that people will have some idea of the musical before actual auditions take place.

Auditions

Each musical society will have their own unique way of doing things, but generally speaking people applying for principal parts will be invited to sing appropriate set pieces from the musical to demonstrate their ability and whether they are right for the part. Members of the chorus will also audition, but in their case it is to determine the vocal range and harmonies so they will be correctly positioned within the chorus.

The auditions will take place in front of a producer, musical director and, if applicable, choreographer. There may be at least two committee members present to supply independent advice.

Casting

It is worth pointing out that musical societies have different ways of doing things regarding casting. In some societies the producer has the final say, taking into consideration the views of his colleagues. A musical director is there to consider the actor's musical ability and similarly the choreographer is there to make a judgement about potential dancing ability. The committee members may make a contribution about the person as an individual if there's anything of which the producer needs to be aware. In this scenario, the producer has the final say, with rubber-stamping from the committee.

However, there are other societies where it is the committee who does the actual casting. Producers and musical directors can sometimes be paid professionals and, as such, not members of the society *per se*. While they can make suggestions as to casting, the committee will make the decision, leaving the producer and musical director with a cast they may not necessarily perceive as the best.

The committee has many considerations, the most significant of which is to make sure the show is a financial success. This is very important, of course, but can lead to conservative and static casting. During the course of writing this book I have been privy to many off-the-record comments, some of which are consistent grievances, among which is the case where the die is cast in typecasting. If you get a principal part soon after joining a society then you are considered a principal player for future productions. If you are cast in the chorus it is difficult to escape the chorus with that society, unless death or mishap befalls a principal actor. Even then some societies may engage in an arrangement with another society who have recently performed the musical and get their respective principal to replace their own principal if rehearsals are under way or performances are imminent.

From a casting point of view there are legitimate technical reasons for this, for example, in G&S musicals the main lead is written for a soprano because Gilbert & Sullivan originally wrote the part for a particular actor. On the other hand, a common complaint is that the accomplished lead is always cast as such even when they are too old for the part (which plays into the hands of stereotyping in amateur theatre by the public) and this frustrates younger members of the society. However, there may be legitimate concerns as to whether new and younger performers have the stamina, energy and skill to undertake these demanding roles, particularly if a matinée and evening performance are scheduled in the run.

If you perceive that the society is stagnating and limiting opportunity, this could be your cue to either join another society or try and get on the committee and take responsibility for changing things. A change in personnel in key positions on the committee, or a change of musical director can make a difference. Before joining a society it may be worth checking on past production cast lists to see if the same names recur in the same roles.

Putting that aside, however, for many people, involvement in regular large-cast musical productions is not about getting principal roles but about the sheer fun of doing a musical, and much fun can be had as part of the chorus.

Engaging professional personnel

On occasion, an amateur company may wish to engage a professional to perform some service for them. Irrespective of whom you are going to pay or what the job is, it is advisable to have a written contract that explicitly states what the group expects from the professional concerned and, likewise, what the professional can expect from the group.

Musical societies are likely to pay for a producer, musical director and musicians, while non-musical groups may well engage a professional director for a given production. There are other theatre practitioners that may be employed, but a written contract is a must to protect both parties.

Without a contract there is no comeback if a musical director walks out halfway through the rehearsal period. To that end, always check the credentials of any professional you may wish to use. The bottom line is that the theatre group or musical society is giving that person a job and, like a business employer, you want to know you are getting the right person for the job.

Ask for references and do check out what a producer or musical director is like. Other groups' experiences can save you a lot of hassle and disappointment in the future. NODA offers its members a model contract for directors, which can be adapted by societies for their own particular circumstances.

Rehearsals

Once the cast has been established rehearsals will begin. For musicals, rehearsals may take up to six months, with the norm being rehearsals once or twice a week.

Rehearsal stage 1: Musical

The first half of the rehearsal period is devoted to musical rehearsals, with the musical director in charge. During these rehearsals it is all about the songs – learning the words, the music and the correct delivery. There will initially be separate rehearsals for the principals and the chorus, before the two elements are merged into a harmonious musical whole.

Rehearsal stage 2: Floor

The second half of the rehearsal period is devoted to the floor rehearsals, where principals and chorus come together to put the visual aspect of the production together under the direction of the producer. Remember, not every word in a musical is sung (there are exceptions) – there will dialogue too. Like a non-musical play, both words and lyrics need to be learned without the book and the same process of blocking (see Chapter 02 The actors) must be gone through to establish moves, entrances and exits. Since musicals are big-cast plays this is no mean feat for any producer. Although it is the music that attracts the audience with those memorable toe-tapping numbers, a producer should never lose sight of the fact that they are telling a story and that theatre is a visual medium, although some producers and actors sometimes regard dialogue as merely a means to get principal A from one part of the stage to another to sing the next song!

For musicals you do need energy, stamina and patience for floor rehearsals because, although enjoyable, they are hard work and everyone has to work together to make the best production possible.

Technical rehearsal

Technical rehearsals are where all the technical aspects come together to make a show. The band or orchestra is often involved for the first time, although some groups hold a band session where band and cast informally play together in a rehearsal room before getting into the theatre auditorium. The lighting, set, sound and any special effects also have to be tested and shown to work. This is a long, frustrating rehearsal session because often the producer and musical director will only learn that what they planned does actually work when it is woven together with the light and sound and other special effects.

Dress rehearsal

This will be the first and, probably, the only time there will be a full, uninterrupted run through of the whole musical before a paying audience sees the show the following evening.

Costumes

For such large-cast productions, costumes are often hired and one consequence of that is that the cast won't see or put on what they are wearing until, at best, a week beforehand, or at the dress rehearsal. There are very often costume sets available for hire, for example, for G&S musicals there is a choice of sets but essentially the design falls within certain design parameters.

These sets can often be sourced from other musical societies, in particular, the theatre-owning societies of the Little Theatre Guild. With hire costumes there is invariably the need for adjustments or even swapping with a fellow cast member. The safety pin is often king!

Another thing for the hardworking wardrobe department to consider (who will be responsible for the sourcing and maintenance of the costumes) is the use of radio microphones. Musical societies sometimes allocate their principal players with radio mics for the performance. The mics may be placed on the costume while the accompanying transmitter pack also needs to be concealed. A conversation with the sound designer and/or engineer should take place before costumes are ordered.

The performance

One advantage of musicals is that they are popular with audiences and you can be assured the show will attract a decent-sized house for each performance. Musicals epitomize 'show business' with big casts, wonderful costumes and popular music, and the performance should be thoroughly enjoyed by cast, crew and audience despite the pre-show nerves.

There may be a matinée scheduled at some point in the run, which will require everyone to be set and ready to do two performances in a day: one in the afternoon and the second in the evening, with only a few hours break in between. On those days it is important to rest and eat properly because both performances need to be as good as each other.

Sound design for musicals

Sound design is very important for musicals, particularly if microphones are used. The sound designer/engineer has to be the ears of the audience for a production. To be fair, there are many venues that do not need the use of microphones, loudspeakers and PA systems because of the way the auditoriums were originally designed.

However, some venues, either through design or sheer size, or a dance-heavy musical, require technological support to give a pleasing sound for the audience. Remember, the sound designer/engineer needs to balance three main sources of sound – the principals, the chorus and the musicians.

Radio microphones are restricted to the principals and are designed to pick up the wearer's voice. The microphone may be placed on the actor's clothing, behind their ear or on top of the temple. For each microphone there will be a transmitter pack that the actor has to wear. This transmitter will need to be concealed within the actor's costume, so a consultation with the wardrobe department or costume designer before costumes are ordered or made will be necessary to make them aware of this issue.

The sound engineer will have to check that the radio mics transmit clearly from all parts of the stage and notify the producer immediately if there is a problem.

The chorus can be boosted by microphones known as floats, which will be on the front edge of the stage and will pick up anyone downstage. Shotgun microphones may be placed in the wings or above the stage to boost the upstage areas on larger stages. The position of these microphones adds another consideration for the producer and cast, who will need to be aware of where they are and not come into contact with them.

For musicians, a sound engineer would probably use condensor microphones, but much depends on the venue and also whether it is better to use amplifiers or a PA system to feed the sound to the audience.

A technique of sound reinforcement is sometimes used to produce a better overall sound – instead of increasing the volume of the whole package it will merely boost the weaker elements in the soundscape.

When it comes down to it, you and the audience will know if it does not sound right.

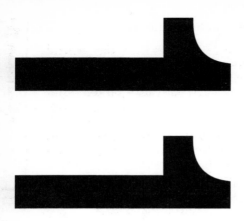

festivals

In this chapter you will learn:

- what drama festivals are
- how to participate in a festival
- how adjudicators and adjudications work.

Types of festival

There are essentially two types of festival – the general arts/drama festival and the competitive festival. The first will allow your company to perform a work in, perhaps, a new venue. You may have an existing play that has been successful on home turf and you may feel it would be popular elsewhere and choose to do additional performances as part of a festival. In this situation, always check with the festival organizers as well as the venue in which you will be performing. Always budget for festivals and seriously consider what your potential income will be from any performances. Additional marketing may be required as well as transport costs for cast, crew and set.

Competitive festivals are where various amateur groups come together and perform their show of either a one-act or full-length play. An independent adjudicator will mark and compare each performance before the winning production is announced. There are usually supplementary awards for best actor, best director and so on.

The most prominent of the festival organizers are the All England Theatre Festival (AETF), Drama Association of Wales, Scottish Community Drama Association and the Association of Ulster Drama Associations. These four organizations have a pyramid system for one-act plays that leads to the naming of annual national champions, who then compete for the overall British title.

Another prominent festival organizer is the National Drama Festival Association (NDFA) that runs 18 full-length play festivals and 44 one-act play festivals. Like the AETF events, there is a pyramid from local to national finals and, ultimately, the British All Winners Festival which is a week-long celebration of theatre.

A one-act play can run between 20 and 55 minutes in performance, but it also can be an excerpt from a longer play, provided that it is coherent as a self-contained piece of drama for the audience and that the appropriate permission has been gained from the author or the author's agents.

Under the AETF, England is split into four organising areas, namely, Central, Eastern, Northern and Western. Within these areas are geographical sub-divisions in which a series of festivals will take place. For example, the Northern section is split into three areas: North West, North Central and North East. Within the North West region there could be festivals held in Cumbria, West Pennines, Mersey, Dee and Bolton and Manx. The winners from these festivals would go on to compete in a divisional final. The winner of the divisional final will then go on to represent the North West in the Northern area final, the winner of which will in turn go on to represent the Northern area in the English final. The English champions then go on to compete against the Scottish, Ulster and Welsh champions for the British title.

All these festivals are under the auspices of the AETF, or independent festival organizers who have been approved by the AETF committee. As mentioned previously, the NDFA runs a similar event.

Each festival is hosted by one venue, so all productions perform on the same stage. There are strict rules regarding performance with a time limit (20–55 minutes) and the adjudicator can penalize a group if the performance overruns or is seriously short. There are time limits for building (10 minutes) and striking the set (5 minutes). This is particularly the case for one-act festivals where there could be three or four companies performing in the same session.

How to enter

To enter a festival your drama group will need to submit an official entry form, which usually asks for the name of the company and the play you wish to perform. Many festival organizers have the rules (which you will need a copy of) on their website and a downloadable entry form. A non-refundable entry fee will be required at this time. Also, you will need to make clear that if your society is selected as the winner it would be willing to carry on to the next stage. It is worth noting that the further you go in the competition, the further afield you are likely to have to travel, for example, the 2006 AETF Champions were St Ursula Players from Bristol who featured in the English final at Hereford's Courtyard Theatre and contested the British Final at the Perth Theatre in Perth, Scotland.

Once your entry has been accepted – and sometimes they can be refused because of the nature of the play you wish to perform, or oversubscription to the festival, or black listing due to past behaviour – the festival organizers will require a copy of the script and the appropriate performance licence as well as the music rights, if applicable. If any amendments have been made to the script, for example, to accommodate the time limit on performance, the organizers will require the express written permission of the author to prove that you are allowed to make the changes. Failure to fulfil any of these requirements can lead to a refusal to allow you to perform. Apart from the loss of the deposit and the disappointment of your company, the festival hosts will also be put out as they will not want a blank session on their programme.

There may be occasions when a company has to withdraw from a festival, but if the reason given for the cancellation is not satisfactory it may lead to blacklisting in future years. Even if your lead actor is out, a performance will still be expected by the organizers, even if this means someone else stepping into the role and having to read from the script on stage. There are contractual obligations. By all means discuss with the organizers what they expect if any scenario should occur that leads to a potential cancellation.

Before the festival begins, the organizers will expect a representative from your group – usually the stage manager – to liaise with the festival's technical manager and inform and arrange the technical aspects of the show.

Although you may wish to submit certain information that expresses a preference for a certain time in the schedule, once the festival committee has allocated your slot it is extremely unlikely to be changed. Some festival organizers use the drawing of lots as the fairest way of allocating the performance times. There are other considerations such as balancing the programme in terms of genre or themes and also running times. Having one night's performances finish at 9.30pm and the following night's at 11.30pm is not good theatre programming for organizers, adjudicators, drama societies or the audience.

Once the plays have been performed the adjudicator – usually GoDA registered (see below) – will verbally announce the winners (but not the marks). It will be a condition of entry that your group must be represented at the awards ceremony. If your group wants a written adjudication this must be requested and an additional fee paid.

Guild of Drama Adjudicators (GoDA)

The AEFT and NDFA normally use adjudicators from the Guild of Drama Adjudicators. To become a member of GoDA the applicant will undertake a two-year mentoring period with an experienced adjudicator before becoming an associate, then, after six official adjudications, they will become a full adjudicator. An annual selection weekend, which features instruction and testing elements, determines who will be accepted to embark on the mentoring period.

An adjudicator should give a well-structured and understandable verbal judgement. He/she needs to have experience, ideally of both professional and amateur theatre. They have to read all the scripts submitted and accepted by the festival and have knowledge of both plays and playwrights. AETF or NDFA festivals, at their various stages, can be anything from a weekend to a week-long affair, with two or three performance sessions in a day.

When appointing a GoDA adjudicator the festival organizers will need to negotiate a fee. GoDA only sets a minimum fee per session for its members, which is merely a starting point for the negotiations between the festival and the individual adjudicator. If a written adjudication is required by any drama group, then they have to approach the adjudicator directly before the event and pay an additional fee.

If you do get a written adjudication it is worth noting how the marks are calculated: acting 40%, production 35%, stage presentation 15% and dramatic achievement 10%. There will be an overall category mark of A (75+), B (60–74), C (40–59) and D (under 40) which equates to very good, good, fair and poor.

GoDA, to its credit, does assess its member adjudicators, encouraging festival organizers to submit their confidential comments. It has to be noted that GoDA will not entertain submissions from participating companies or individuals about their members – only comments from festival organizers will be considered.

There are other independent adjudicators who also adjudicate at festivals.

Case study

St Ursula Players

The St Ursula Players were the 2006 All England Theatre Festival One-Act Drama Festival Champions with their production of *Me and My Friend* by Gillian Plowman. Below is an interview with the winning director, Marie O'Sullivan, about the one-act drama experience.

Q: Why enter a competitive drama festival?

Marie: There are several very good reasons for entering a one-act drama festival. Firstly, it enables our directors to work on more demanding texts than they would otherwise be able to in our own 'home' venues, as some material could be unsuitable for our local audiences, or they would not attract large enough audiences to make the production financially viable. In a festival, there are usually three plays on each evening and, therefore, the ticket selling responsibility is spread.

Secondly, my group uses the festival to bring on new directors and give actors the opportunity to play roles they might not get the opportunity to play in a full-length production. We have also used festivals to give young people in the group the opportunity to perform in plays that are particularly suitable for them. In other words, festivals are an important training ground for both experienced and inexperienced directors and actors alike, to enhance their creative skills and to explore more challenging work.

Festivals are also very demanding on the backstage crew: designing a believable setting that can be put up in ten minutes and struck in five, and which can be effective in any type of performance venue. Festivals also provide the experience of working in a new environment, often with a professional stage crew.

Q: How do you go about selecting the play and personnel?

Marie: The choice of play is largely in the hands of the director, who then submits his/her choice to the committee for approval. Being committed to an ensemble type of club, we would always choose a play to fit the availability of members, at the same time encouraging the team to explore new themes, controversial styles, or less accessible work by such playwrights as Pinter, Beckett or Stoppard.

For those groups who are fortunate enough to have an 'in house' playwright, the opportunity can be taken in a one-act festival to give an 'original play' an airing, which might be risky as a full-length option. Occasionally, some members cannot commit to the extended rehearsal period that a full-length play demands, so the shorter rehearsal time for a one-act play is preferable for them.

Q: When did you begin rehearsing?

Marie: The Bristol Festival is usually held during either the second or third week in February. For the 2006 Festival, I whittled the choice down to three plays that I felt I could cast with those members I had available. Ultimately I decided that I could get the strongest production out of *Me and My Friend* by Gillian Plowman, which had a cast of two men, and this selection was done before Christmas 2005. We had a break for Christmas and the New Year and rehearsals started on Wednesday, 4th January.

Due to a change of festival venue, the festival was held a week later than usual, which worked in our favour as I lost a week of rehearsals due to one of the cast being away. However, I was still able to get in six weeks of rehearsals – two rehearsals a week, which is what I would usually allow for a one-act play. (When planning a January schedule, the director has to bear in mind that coughs and colds can play havoc with rehearsals at that time of the year!)

Q: How did you keep the production fresh for occasional competitive performances from February to June/July?

Marie: We have been fortunate enough to have had a lot of experience in keeping productions fresh through several festival rounds. I am sure most directors would agree that, after the first round, there is still work to be done and it is vitally important to keep re-assessing your work and looking at ways it can be improved – it must never get boring or dull.

Q: Was there any constructive criticism in your winning adjudications that saw you change or improve things for the next round?

Marie: Personally, I would always have a written adjudication mainly because it gives the director and cast the opportunity to sit down and quietly assimilate a qualified adjudicator's comments, rather than everyone chipping in with what they thought the adjudicator said from the stage. We were fortunate enough to have had four of the most experienced adjudicators assessing our production prior to the British final, and while we did not always agree with everything they said, we took something away from each of them which certainly enhanced our performance – and this is another important way of keeping the production fresh. I would always advise trying out any suggestions made by an adjudicator in rehearsals to see if their suggestions work for your production – bearing in mind that this is *your* production and *your* ideas.

Q: Is there an added pressure in your performance because it is a competition?

Marie: Many people do not like competitive drama and I do understand this, however, personally, I feel that the 'edge' a competition gives is an enhancement – it keeps you on your toes. You are often playing in a venue which is new to you, often in the semi-round, which is always a challenge, and in front of a new audience and, hopefully, you could be acquiring a new following. I like to think that any performance we give is to the best of our ability, be it in a festival or on our home ground, and I would expect us to rise to the challenge of any performance no matter where it is given.

Q: How, if at all, do the drama festivals affect the rest of your programme?

Marie: Fitting in a festival can be tricky for many clubs, especially those who do a pantomime, however, we perform two three-act plays a year and these we do in the beginning of December and in April (depending when Easter falls), which tends to fit in well with the festival scene. The one real problem when starting out, is that we do not know whether we will be required to go forward to the next round (which is usually held in April in our area), so to cover this eventuality we try not to overlap the cast with the spring production, but very often we have had to double up on the stage crew. In some years we have had to ask for an afternoon performance in the divisional final, so that the crew can get back to Bristol in time for the evening performance of the spring show!

Q: What are the good points of entering a competitive drama festival?

Marie: After over 30 years of directing and performing in festival plays, I still feel I am learning all the time and, looking back on the wonderful experiences we have had and the beautiful venues we have played in, I feel we have been very privileged to have been part of an exciting and stimulating scene. Also, a festival gives the opportunity to see other groups perform and to learn from their adjudications, particularly in the later rounds when the standard is so very high. It also affords the opportunity to meet other enthusiasts who share the same love of theatre.

Q: What are the negative points of entering a drama festival?

Marie: I can't really think of any negative points of entering a drama festival! I would only say that it does need very careful organization, particularly as we have to remember that our full-length plays in our own 'homes' are our 'bread and butter'.

Q: How do you budget for such an event? Presumably, you don't expect to reach the British final and with each round there are ever increasing travel and accommodation costs?

Marie: The basic costs come out of club funds. Happily, throughout most rounds a raffle is held and the proceeds are given to the winning club to offset the costs of the next round; it never covers everything, but it certainly is a help. Our members pay their own expenses, but if there is anything left in the 'kitty' then members can apply for a 'sub'.

I would just like to add that for any group wishing to hone their creative theatrical skills, there is no finer learning ground than a one-act drama festival.

Case study

Greater Manchester Drama Festival (GMDF)

The Greater Manchester Drama Festival is one of the largest – if not the largest – drama festival not only in Britain but in Europe. The GMDF has over 70 society members in the Greater Manchester area that can enter their productions into the different categories for which the GMDF gives awards. GMDF has three overall sections:

Section A – full-length plays of at least two acts under the direction of one person.

Section B – other full-length productions such as musicals and pantomimes.

Section C – full-length plays from societies awarded the GMDF Drama Shield over the previous ten years.

Approximately 120 different productions take part in the festival (compared with only five in the very first festival back in 1944). The festival season runs from September to June, with societies submitting as many different productions as they wish. Each section is overseen by a single adjudicator, who will see every production entered (which can be up to 45 different productions) and determine the winners accordingly. The festival climaxes with an awards night in late June. The winners are eligible to take part in the NDFA All Winners Festival.

In addition, the GMDF also runs a one-act drama festival in June, which is open to all its members and in alternate years non-member societies from elsewhere can also enter. However, the week-long event has limited spaces with a first come, first served policy in place for the entrants. The one-act drama festival also includes junior and youth sections. Furthermore, the winners can go on to the NDFA All Winners Festival.

GMDF adjudicators

'The adjudicator needs to command the respect of the members of the societies they are visiting. We look for people with knowledge and experience. It is no good appointing an adjudicator if the membership thinks they talk a load of rubbish.'

Cyril Hines, GMDF Chairman

'There are some very, very good societies and some very inexperienced societies, but what I look for is the respect for the work they are presenting and for them to approach it very seriously. They need to be as professional as they possibly can within their capabilities.

'It is important, as well, not to colour your judgement, whether you're going to see a village hall production or you're going to some splendid theatre. It is a blank page when you get there, wherever the venue is.

'Adjudications are there to improve standards. Theatre could die very easily otherwise, but if you can improve standards then audiences will appreciate that, they will keep their hobby and theatre alive.'

Meg Bray, GMDF Adjudicator

'You have got to view everybody across the broad spectrum so that there is an equal playing field for them all to be assessed on, but you've also got to view them within their own capability, facility, money available, resources. If you do that it means the little girl on the church hall stage with just a piano and a few curtains around her can present a song in character which is comparable with someone who performs with a society at the Opera House in Manchester in a similar part who isn't as good. That's how the festival should work. It means there should be a standard and a quality that maps across every production.

'The disheartening thing is when you've adjudicated the same section for three, four, five seasons and you see the same correctable mistakes being made every year, which suggests people don't learn from experience and they are only in it to see if they can win a gong.

'It should be about entering this community of theatre and developing within it, making theatre live and possibly making it successful.

'The festival is successful because it is respected and the product that we produce is of use and, even though we don't want it to be perceived by the members as just about winning an award, if that keeps them going and makes them get involved in the festival then there is a spin-off from it and the spin-off is that they might improve what they do, and if they improve what they do the public is more interested in amateur theatre and it becomes self-perpetuating.'

Martin Roche, GMDF Adjudicator

'What disappoints me is when they don't have an adjudication to find out why they haven't won the trophy when probably they think they should have done. More importantly, they need to know why they are good, why they won that, what they did to be awarded that. To be able to follow any sort of path and say that was right so we must carry on being right or that was wrong, we must correct the wrong and perhaps go that way. People who think they don't need to be told whether they are right, wrong, good, indifferent or bad but quite happy to take the trophies and say we were good but we don't know why we were good.

'An adjudication is still somebody else's opinion at the end of the day and we're all free to choose not to accept it or disagree with it, that is human nature, but if you're still respectful to be able to see it, acknowledge it as a piece of work that somebody has done.'

Sue Mooney, GMDF Secretary

part

two

community theatre:
from registration to
rehearsal

12

setting up a new community theatre group

In this chapter you will learn:
- how to set up a community theatre group
- how to write a constitution
- how to create criteria for membership and elect officers
- who the elected officers of the committee are and their responsibilities
- how to utilize the membership to aid the committee.

Forming a theatre group

So, you want to set up your own community theatre group? Your best resource for this is other theatre groups who possess much experience in the running and maintenance of amateur companies. You could probably contact them directly via websites and see if anyone is willing to help or advise you on avoiding pitfalls. Features and forum sections of the www.amdram.co.uk website could be a good resource, but beware of conflicting advice and be aware that there are, on occasions, regional differences that affect amateur groups. Certainly there are legal differences in Northern Ireland and Scotland from England and Wales. There are, of course, organizations such as NODA that may help. This chapter is designed to offer a guide to setting up your own amateur group.

First, you need a group of like-minded individuals. You may already have friends who want to help you create this group. Alternatively, you could publicize your intention to set up a new theatre group and see who responds. You will need also to determine what kind of productions you would like to stage. You may decide that you want to stage only plays or pantomimes or musicals. Within those categories you may wish to specialize and solely perform Shakespeare plays or become a Gilbert & Sullivan society (both canons of work have the benefit of being out of copyright), or perform only Ayckbourn comedies or straight plays, or you may be willing to try all genres. From the outset it is a good idea to create a mission statement, which will give focus to your group.

Theatre group status

The National Operatic and Dramatic Association (NODA) believes many community theatre groups, when ascertaining their legal status, should consider the option of a Charitable Company Limited by Guarantee. There are many benefits to becoming such a legal organization, not least of which are financial and security advantages for the group and its members. We will first look at the forming of a Company Limited by Guarantee and the benefits of doing so. We will then examine how to achieve charitable status.

Company Limited by Guarantee

Non-profit-making organizations such as community theatre groups – they do make profits, but these are always invested into future productions and maintenance of the group, not paid to shareholders – can become a Company Limited by Guarantee. What this means is that the organization acquires a legal status separate from its members and, generally, members will not be liable for any significant debts if, in the worst-case scenario, the group has to be wound up owing money. In that case, members would be legally obliged to pay between £1 and £5 to creditors.

Members of a Company Limited by Guarantee are entitled to voting rights at the group's Annual General Meeting and any Extraordinary General Meetings. They will be responsible, by ballot, for the election and removal of directors (who form the committee) and will also determine any fundamental change to the group's status and/or rules. There must be a register of all existing members on record at the group's registered office.

In terms of maintenance, it is important that accounts are audited and sent to Companies House and all statutory records, such as membership lists, are kept up to date.

The committee

The committee (i.e. the board of directors) must be elected by the group's membership and, if the group is also intending to be a registered charity, no member of the committee should be paid.

Every member of the committee must comprehend and be committed to the purpose of the group. The committee must meet at least four times a year. In reality, most amateur theatre groups' committees meet at least once month, so this should not be a problem.

The committee is financially and legally responsible for the group and the members can, if they act irresponsibly or maliciously, be liable for debts incurred as a result of their actions in 'wrongful trading'. At all times they must have up-to-date financial records and information and make sure the theatre group's transactions are correctly applied and within the remit of its operations. Ideally, a solicitor or an accountant should be a member of the committee, to keep matters in check.

See the section on the constitution, below, for details on the selection of committee members.

The committee, at any given time, can be supplemented by other members of the group if those members have information or contributions that can help the committee make informed decisions. However, these seconded members should not have their contributions recorded in the minutes or indeed be allowed to vote on committee decisions.

Those are the obligations of the committee and the members when a Company Limited by Guarantee is formed. To attain this coveted status, the group will need to create a Memorandum and Articles of Association, that is, a constitution (see page 114).

Committee members

Chairman

The chairman will oversee and participate in committee meetings and be familiar with the group's own written constitution. He/she makes representations on behalf of the committee but does not agree to anything without the committee's approval. In many groups the chairman is a signatory for cheques and accessing the group's bank account and may be given the casting vote on the committee in the event of a deadlock.

Vice-chairman

The vice-chairman is there to aid the chairman in their duties and should be prepared to step into his/her place when the chairman is not available. This role may be specifically elected by the membership or by a vote within the committee.

Secretary

The secretary is a pivotal member of the society and needs to possess excellent organizational, administrative and record-keeping skills. The secretary can be responsible for taking the minutes of the meetings (unless a minute secretary has been appointed) and arranging venues for various activities of the society. They will also communicate to the members the key decisions of the committee, usually via a monthly newsletter and/or email.

Treasurer

This role carries enormous responsibility as the treasurer oversees the group's finances, maintaining the accounts and keeping the committee regularly informed of these. The treasurer has to submit an annual statement of accounts at the end of the financial year, with a copy made available to all the members.

Membership secretary

This role is initially to act as a contact point for new members. This may necessitate the publication of the membership secretary's telephone number in programmes, media articles and online. The membership secretary should investigate and initiate ways of attracting new members to the society. They should also maintain the existing membership list and ensure that subscription fees are up to date, although this responsibility does on occasion pass to the secretary or the treasurer.

Publicity officer

This person will be the point of contact for media enquiries and needs to know who are the relevant journalists, editors, photographers and broadcasters. The publicity officer needs to be aware of the various deadlines for submitting press releases and/or photographs when promoting the group's activities and its latest production.

They also will be responsible for the promotion of both the group and its activities. They will be responsible for the design and printing of all literature, seeking approval from both the committee and the members who are the subject of such publicity while aiming to give the society maximum exposure. The role may be split between two members.

Business manager

A business manager oversees the on-going expenditure of a given project and makes sure all the necessary arrangements and appropriate contracts are signed – including engaging professional personnel. They will keep records and make recommendations for improved practice.

Solicitor

It would be wise for any society to have the services of a named solicitor on hand either on the committee (if you're fortunate) or available for consultation regarding any legal issues that may arise within or concerning the society.

Social secretary

The social secretary is responsible for sourcing and arranging extra-curricular social activities for the benefit of the membership away from the staging of shows.

Play-reading team

All community theatre groups need to find plays or musicals to stage. A dedicated team devoted to sourcing and reading scripts for recommendation to the committee offers a combined service and social activity for the group. The readers do not have to be committee members.

The constitution

Naming the group

The constitution document must include the name of the group. At this point it is worth mentioning that the name of your group may be affected by charity status. That is, the Charity Commission will not duplicate charitable organizations' names on its register, so if the name you choose is already being used elsewhere by another charity you will be unable to use that name. This is not a problem for the vast majority of community theatre groups, because most groups trade on their locality, and the name of their town or neighbourhood is usually incorporated into the group's name. Just think of how many Gilbert & Sullivan Operatic Societies there are in the country. What gives them their identity is their location.

The name should reflect what the group is about by making it clear whether you are a musical, theatrical or youth group, for example: Peterborough Mask Theatre, Abbey Musical Society, Pinner Gilbert & Sullivan Operatic Society or Ashbourne Youth Theatre. Some groups have deliberately created a memorable acronym for their group, such as Hordern Amateur Theatrical Society (HATS), Colnbrook Amateur Stage Theatre (CAST), Longsdon Amateur Dramatic Society (LADS) or Children's Amateur Theatre Society (C-A-T-S).

Objects

Along with the name, the group will need to state their objects. This formal declaration as part of the constitution is important because it could help the group to attain charitable status. NODA produces a model constitution to help groups create their own constitution. In this model, under the heading of 'Objects', the constitution reads: 'The objects of the Society are to educate the public in the dramatic and operatic arts, and to further the development of public appreciation and taste in the said arts.'

Some established community theatre groups publish their constitution on their websites and it is worth looking at them. Gosforth Amateur Dramatic Society (GADS) declares its objects as follows: 'the production of dramatic art and encouragement of theatre appreciation and in the pursuance of such objects to give performances of dramatic works and to promote such other activities as shall conduce to the fulfilment of the above general objects.'

Leighton Buzzard Drama Group has a more simply worded object, which states that, 'The Object of the Group shall be to encourage and provide opportunity for the enjoyment of the Dramatic Arts.'

Executive committee

Several criteria need to be established regarding the executive committee (the committee), as follows:

- number of executive officials
- election of officials
- term of office
- voting procedures for committee decision-making.

The constitution will need to establish the make-up of the executive committee. The three must-have officials are chairman, secretary and treasurer. The usual form is for the chairman, secretary and treasurer to be elected specifically for these posts. Other committee members – the number of which can vary (usually about five) and will be decided upon by the group and written into the constitution – will be elected and their responsibilities determined within the committee. The committee is ultimately responsible for the direction, well-being and prosperity of the group.

The majority of committee members should be elected by the membership for a fixed term of office, although there is no reason why non-voting members of the group cannot be seconded to aid and support committee members for specific projects. How this is determined will be for each individual group to decide. Those members who ask to undertake such tasks should at least be overseen by or report to a named committee member.

It should be established how the election process takes place. The Annual General Meeting is often used for the election, with members either volunteering or being formally nominated for the various posts available. The member who gains the most votes in a given category, for example, chairman, will be elected to the role.

The 'term of office' for each member will need to be established. Individual groups will have to decide for themselves the duration of each officer's term. Two years is the common period of office in many groups. After two years, the official concerned can step down or seek re-election.

It is good practice to stagger the elections for individual executive committee posts. For example, if the committee is made up of eight people, including chairman, secretary and treasurer, then half of the officials should stand for election at any one time. So, one year, four committee member posts will be contested in the election, and each member will be elected for two years. The following year, the other four posts will be contested. In this way the group should never lose the committee *en masse* (which would be a disaster), and will provide continuity and ensure that there are always experienced members on the committee.

There should be a clear statement in the constitution regarding the powers and responsibilities of the committee. It should also be determined how decisions are made within the committee structure. For example, is a motion carried simply by a majority verdict, or does a minimum number of committee members need to support a decision before it is carried?

Quorum

What is known as a quorum must be established within the constitution, in relation to any decision-making process, either at committee level or membership level at the AGM. A quorum is the minimum number of members required at a committee meeting or the AGM before any official decision-making can occur. This is designed to prevent the few acting against the wishes of the majority.

Since memberships vary in size from year to year, the quorum may be determined by a percentage figure, for example, at the AGM 25 or 30 per cent of the membership must attend. At committee level, a majority numerical figure needs to be established, for example, on a committee of eight the quorum could be five, or on a committee of 12 the quorum could be seven. Attendance below that figure will prevent any official business being enacted on behalf of the theatre group.

Membership

Who is eligible?

The issue of who can become a member needs to be established. For example, there may be a minimum or maximum age limit. A community theatre children's or youth group may have a minimum age of five years old and a maximum of 14, 16, 18 or 21. An adult amateur group may set a minimum age of 16 or 18. Other groups will have an open policy with no age restrictions.

How do people join and what fees would members pay?

Some groups, like musical societies, may only accept a new member after a satisfactory audition. There may be an entrance and/or subscription fee with a potential new member only being accepted if the applicant has filled in an application form and paid the appropriate fees. Some societies may give a new member a limited period of grace before the subscription fee is requested. Non-payment, of course, results in non-membership. All this needs to be explicit in the constitution.

Registration as a Company Limited by Guarantee

The group will need a registered office, which may be a member's address or, for a fee, it can be a solicitor. The advantage of the latter is that the group's solicitor will probably be a constant while members can and do change, which will require Companies House being informed of a change of registered office. There may be a fee involved for any change of details to the company.

A number of forms will need to be completed and signed by a solicitor, and a standard registration fee will need to be paid. Becoming a limited company can be a complicated process and legal advice is required. Company law has to be adhered to and administered, but once limited liability is established it opens the door for the group to begin trading and, where necessary, employ professionals. The group becomes a legal entity that can initiate or be the subject of legal action. Most importantly, it gives a welcome security to the group and its members.

Societies can become Companies Limited by Guarantee without registering as a charity, which would allow them to employ and pay a number of executive members.

An application form, a copy of the Memorandum and Articles of Association, the constitution and the appropriate fee must be sent to Companies House. Then, within 14 days, the group will become a Company Limited by Guarantee.

Addresses

England and Wales: Companies House, Crown Way, Cardiff CF4 3UZ Tel: 0870 333 3636

Scotland: Companies House, 37 Castle Street, Edinburgh HE1 2EB Tel: 0131 535 5800

Northern Ireland*: The Companies Registry, IDB House, 64 Chichester Street, Belfast BT1 4JX Tel: 028 90 234 488

*Companies in Northern Ireland have a separate legal identity and its members are not normally legally responsible for debts incurred. The responsibilities of directors in Northern Ireland are outlined in the 1986 and 1990 Companies (NI) Orders. The public Companies Register will have companies' details while accounts must include a balance sheet and profit and loss account for each financial year.

The company will be registered by the completion of the Companies Register forms 21 and 23, along with the appropriate fee, and a check will be done on the name of the group to make sure it does not already exist.

Case study

Chairman

Within four years of joining her local community theatre group Diana Mortimer became the group's chairman. She showed there was nothing to fear while imposing her own style on a well-established committee.

'I only joined the committee last year and I thought it would be fun because I was getting a lot out of the Mask Theatre. I wanted to put something back in and I knew that it had been through harder times than it would have liked to have been in the last few years. I thought, yes, I would like to get involved and show I had that commitment to the organization.

'I wanted to learn how it works and there were opportunities to make suggestions as to what we do next or how we might take things forward... I knew there were people like the outgoing chairman Rich Unwin, who weren't on the committee any more, whom I could turn to if something goes wrong and he would give me sage words of advice. Similarly, having John Crisp as treasurer still on the committee dealing with all that finance stuff, which I don't have a clue on basically, was a big help.

'I do tend to drive the committee a bit harder and faster than they've been use to in the past. That is often driven by other things that we want to do. For example, if we had an extended costume meeting at the end of the main meeting that means we can drive through the committee efficiently and I do tend to focus people and keep them running to the agenda. I don't like sitting there listening to people bleating.'

Case study

Business manager

Edward Matty is business manager of West Bromwich Operatic Society. His job is to create and strictly maintain the production budget. It costs an enormous amount of money to stage a musical, for example, West Bromwich OS's production of *The Witches of Eastwick* cost £61,000 to stage.

'Popular musicals are the ones that make money and a popular show is usually determined by whether it was a success in London.

Shows such as *Evita*, *Jesus Christ Superstar* and *Jekyll and Hyde* have all been good for us and everywhere else,' said Edward.

West Bromwich OS usually gives seven performances, including two matinées, in a run that begin on a Tuesday and end on a Saturday. Ticket sales are important and strict adherence to the budget is very important.

'Artistic people can have great ideas but do not necessarily ask whether an item is absolutely necessary or be aware of how much it costs!'

West Bromwich OS employs a producer, musical director and an orchestra paid at Musician Union rates. For auditions the producer, musical director and choreographer will be joined by two committee members who will pass on comments to help with the casting process.

West Bromwich OS also safeguards its productions with coverage for the potential loss of principal actors. First, they will see which other societies have staged the production recently and approach the principals to see if they would be willing to step in if the worst-case scenario befell a production and a leading actor was unable to perform. Due consideration must be given to the distance the actor may have to travel. West Bromwich OS has, on occasion, successfully contacted musical societies as far afield as Bristol with such an arrangement. West Bromwich OS also uses understudies for the parts, just in case an accident should befall a principal on the night.

Charitable status

Once Company by Limited Guarantee status has been established, community theatre groups may consider attaining charity status, although for many groups it is not suitable, particularly since the threshold for turnover is £10,000.

There are enormous benefits to becoming a charity, which include improved opportunities when seeking funding and sponsorship, while the gift-aid scheme will allow donors to donate more money to your group. There is exemption from income tax and corporation tax, plus other tax relief, with theatre-owning societies receiving a mandatory rate relief of 80 per cent.

For a community theatre group to become a charity, the objects declared in its constitution must be seen as appropriately charitable by the law. In this case the law is the Charity Commission and the Inland Revenue. Arts organizations such as community theatre groups need their work to be seen as beneficial to the community at large, for example, through education or encouraging participation in the arts – the work needs to be of 'high artistic merit' and not merely entertainment for entertainment's sake.

The NODA model constitution gives a good example of a society's stated objects that meet charitable status requirements: 'The objects of the Society are to educate the public in the dramatic and operatic arts, and to further the development of public appreciation and taste in said arts.'

A group could gain charitable status if it's objects were to propose the relief of poverty or the advancement of religion.

Charities are run by trustees who, in this case, will be the theatre group's committee members. As with the status of a Company by Limited Guarantee, the committee must act in the interests of the stated objects of the charity. No member must allow any personal interest to overcome the primary aims of the trustees (committee). The objects of the charitable community theatre group are paramount.

To become a charity your community theatre group must register with the Charity Commission and, before submitting an application, it will be in the best interests of the group to consult with the Charity Commissioners. A questionnaire will have to be completed and submitted with two copies of the draft 'governing instrument' (i.e. the constitution) and the group's financial records. The commissioners will consult with the Inland Revenue and may suggest changes to the group's governing instrument and may also advise a change of name if the same name is already registered.

Once the application has been approved, your group can set up as a charity. The completed application form with a certified copy of the governing instrument should then be submitted. The group will be allocated a charity registered number which should be quoted on all correspondence.

Addresses

England: Charity Commission, 12 Princes Dock, Princes Parade, Liverpool L3 1DE (actual/expected income below £10,000) Tel: 0845 3000 218

Charity Commission, Woodfield House, Tangier, Taunton, Somerset TA1 4BC (actual/expected income over £10,000) Tel: 0845 3000 218

Wales: Charity Commission, 8th Floor, Clarence House, Clarence Place, Newport, South Wales NP19 7AA Tel: 0845 3000 218

Scotland*: The Inland Revenue, Financial Intermediaries and Claims Office, Trinity Park House, South Trinity Road, Edinburgh EH5 3SD Tel: 0131 551 8127

*In Scotland, a draft – and appropriately worded – constitution stating the group's charitable aims needs to be submitted to the Inland Revenue's Intermediaries and Claims Office before formally applying.

Northern Ireland: in Northern Ireland you need to apply to the Inland Revenue for charitable status for tax purposes. A written governing instrument stating the group's purpose and how it will run will be required. The Inland Revenue will allocate you a number that either begins XO, XN or XR (this is not a charity registration). Other useful addresses for information and advice:

Charities Branch, Voluntary Activity Unit, Department of Health and Social Services, Castle Buildings, Stormont, Belfast BT4 3PP

Northern Ireland Council for Voluntary Action, 127–131 Ormeau Road, Belfast BT7 1SH

Northern Ireland Voluntary Trust, 22 Mount Charles, Belfast BT7 1NZ

For further information log on to www.charity-commission.gov.uk/registration.

13

budgeting and fundraising

In this chapter you will learn:
- how to prepare a realistic budget
- about costs and potential income
- how to raise and source funds for your theatre group
- the best approach to sponsorship and grants.

The budget

Budget is all. Although community theatre groups do not exist to make a profit *per se*, the bigger the profit on a production the more money can be reinvested in future productions. Profit can then be invested in purchasing equipment that, in the long term, can save money. Bigger and better costumes or props or music can be invested into the next bigger production.

It is very important, therefore, to be aware of all the potential costs of your production. Do not be vague, but get actual quotes. Costs may include:

- performance licence(s)
- rehearsal venue hire
- venue hire
- costumes – hiring or materials for making
- set building – wood, metal, hinges, tools, etc.
- scripts
- publicity – posters, press releases
- programmes, tickets
- props – hiring or creating.

The director, who should have a clear vision of the production, will want to know what the potential costs are to realize his/her vision. Once the budget has been set (which should include a contingency for unforeseen costs) it is important to stick to it. The next task, financially speaking, is to work out exactly when the expenses will be paid. 'Pay promptly' is a good motto. It creates good relations with suppliers and your own creative team.

All the expense of the production has to be recovered and so it is wise to assess carefully your potential income. The main source of income will be from the box office. A realistic prediction of expected audience numbers needs to be given. An assessment of previous productions at the chosen venue, as well as plays of a similar ilk that the group has staged, should be a good guide. Always predict conservatively regarding income. High expectations invariably see a shortfall, which will have implications for the society's future repertoire or even its existence.

Fundraising

Staging plays, musicals and/or running your own theatre is an expensive business even when all those involved are volunteers and do it solely for the love of theatre. To continue doing your hobby your society needs the funds to make it happen.

From the outset community theatre groups will have a basic income stream in the form of annual subscriptions. However, this source, apart from being variable from year to year as members come and go, is often accounted for in the administration of the society, with the monthly newsletter the obvious benefit to the members. Members may be asked to pay other fees such as script, rehearsal or audition fees but there are limits to how much individual members may be able to contribute financially.

The main source of income for a community theatre group is through box-office takings. Unfortunately, receipts can never be guaranteed as no one can ever be certain about the success or otherwise of a show. Box-office receipts can vary from production to production and there is always the danger, of course, of making a loss.

With this in mind, theatre groups need to seek out other sources of funding to survive or thrive. Specific fundraising events have historically been the way for many amateur societies and, to be fair, have served them well. These events could be a social, such as a garden party or a dinner or a dance. They may be of a sporting nature, such as a fancy dress football match, fishing tournament or fun run. Other alternatives include auctions and car boot sales. There are a whole host of different events that could be organized – and several may be undertaken during the year – but anything that has minimal costs, minimum risk and will bring in the extra cash is worth pursuing.

- Chingford Amateur & Operatic Society (CADOS) and their Junior Theatre Group staged a women's shoe sale in March 2005.
- Henley Amateur Operatic & Dramatic Society (HADOS) holds an annual fun run that is open to all athletes and raises significant funds for the group.
- The volunteer-run Barn Theatre, home to the Oxted Operatic Society and the Oxted Players, failed in a Lottery application for a theatre extension that was to provide a new bar and refreshment area, a new dressing room, increased wing space

at stage level plus a new wheelchair-friendly toilet and a wheelchair lift from dressing room to stage level. Undaunted, they created their own lottery which ran every month for over four years. Lottery tickets were sold for £1, of which 45 per cent went on prizes with the balance going towards their Barn 2000 fund.

Other sources of income that can help cover your costs and make a higher percentage of the box-office takings into profit might include:

- selling programmes and advertising space
- selling merchandise and refreshments
- finding sponsorship – this is one of the best sources of income as a generous sponsor could help meet a significant percentage of the production's costs
- applying for grants – for special community theatre projects there may be funding available from government sources.

Programmes

The general standard of both professional and amateur theatre programmes is appalling. The lack of thought put into editorial content is the primary sin. The fact is, no one ever needs to buy a theatre programme, so there has to be a worthwhile reason for members of the audience to part with more cash on top of the cost of their theatre ticket.

Never – and I will say this again – never use a theatre programme to explain any aspect of the play or indeed to explain the play. If you have to do that there is something wrong with your production. What happens on stage should be self-contained and self-explanatory. If a programme explanation is necessary, what happens to the poor audience members who haven't bought one?

The way to regard theatre programmes is as a promotional tool for your theatre group. They can be used to attract new members and can include additional features (a bit like a DVD) that will enhance the experience of the play for the audience. These might include cast and crew biographies and photographs, and should definitely include acknowledgements and credits.

Cast and crew biographies and photographs

First, make sure that biographies are all written in the same style. One of the problems with getting cast members to write their own entries is that they will all vary in style and length. Big white (or whatever colour you use) spaces never looks good editorially speaking. So you want a consistent style and length to each entry. The content of biographies should relate to the actor's theatrical persona or to the theme of the play. On no account should anyone write, 'She is married, has two children and a dog called Rover'. People in the group already know this and the audience really doesn't care! That sort of information is only relevant if the play is about motherhood and/or families and/or dogs! And, at all costs, avoid in-house jokes, which the audience won't get (this applies on stage as well).

The other aspect of biographies is photographs. Keep these up to date. There is nothing worse than a picture of Harry that was taken in 1983 and has been in every programme since!

Acknowledgements and credits

Another important aspect of programmes is to correctly credit people with their contribution and, most important of all, spell their name correctly! Tell people what you have done. Tell the director, tell the stage manager, tell the chairman, tell your department head, tell the programme editor and make sure you get due credit for your contribution.

Keep it interesting

Everything in a theatre programme should be of interest, so make sure your chairman writes something interesting in his column. Have a combination of features that relate to the play and the actual art of staging a play. For example, a feature on how the set came into being or how the costumes were designed and made. You're selling theatre and want to attract more than just potential actors – and you may be able to educate some of your members too!

Finally, tell people how they can become involved with the theatre company and where they can get more information (telephone and/or website). Then, of course, tell them what your next production(s) is, along with the when and where it will be staged.

Sponsorship

If you are hoping to receive a donation or sponsorship from an organization, it is very important to make clear what your group is about, what it promotes and who it benefits. This information is essentially what is contained in your constitution.

Sponsorship can be sourced for a specific production, a season of productions, a theatre or a particular event. The approach in all these cases is to examine how much sponsorship you actually need and ask if it would be reasonable for one company or organization to foot the bill. Would more than one sponsor be necessary? Conceivably you may have one main sponsor with several supplementary sponsors all supporting the same production, venue or event.

When approaching the issue of sponsorship, consider why an individual or, most often, companies should sponsor an amateur theatre production. The answer is that they don't have to sponsor anything, even if you are a charity and/or a community group. There is only a finite amount of funding available and your theatre group will be competing against a whole range of other groups, clubs and causes for that same pot of money.

Why should any organization or company want to sponsor a theatrical production? What can you offer such an organization? What is in it for them? Theatre groups need to appeal to companies in a way which shows that their sponsorship will benefit the company as well as the theatre group. Think what the theatre group can offer in return for sponsorship of their latest production.

- There are obvious methods, like the company logo on all publicity material.
- A press article and photograph can be arranged proclaiming the sponsorship deal.
- The company logo could appear on the programme cover and, inside, two pages of editorial could be turned over to the company to promote itself.
- Always give the major sponsor the back cover of a programme for advertising.
- The company's name could be dropped into radio or television interviews (although the former is better because they are often live interviews).
- You could feature the company's website address.

Present companies with a choice of sponsorship packages and create different financial levels that offer varying benefits which are dependent on the level of sponsorship. Different packages could cover a production, a season or calendar year. You may be fortunate to get more than one sponsor, but set a limit – a company's name will be lost in an array of logos and advertising and you certainly won't get the press to do half-a-dozen sponsorship stories.

Case study

Southampton Musical Society

One approach to gaining sponsorship is to create various sponsorship packages that make clear what a potential sponsor may get for their money. An example of this is provided by Southampton Musical Society (SMS). Southampton Musical Society, as you would expect, stages musicals such as *Anything Goes*, *Calamity Jane*, *Carousel*, *42nd Street* and *West Side Story*. These productions are staged at venues in Southampton, Portsmouth and Winchester and, as we know, musicals are very expensive productions to undertake. For their 2007 production of *West Side Story* at the Theatre Royal in Winchester they offered five potential packages for sponsors and displayed them on their website. These packages ranged between sponsorship of the whole production, sponsorship of an individual night and just taking an advertisement in the production programme. They made clear what was on offer, for example, Package One – Full Show Sponsors: for a minimum of £750, SMS offered company artwork on programmes, 12 free tickets and drinks before the show on a Tuesday or Wednesday night, the sponsoring company's display stand in the foyer of the theatre all week, a full-page advertisement in the programme and the sponsoring company's name featured on all press releases.

SMS also made it explicit why they needed the money: the show cost over £18,000 to stage and the box-office receipts alone would not cover the costs. In general terms they also showed where the money was going, i.e. royalties, sets, costume (£6,000), theatre rental (£5,500) and musical support (£4,500). This kind of detailed information is the key to unlocking any potential sponsorship deal. Any sponsoring organization or company will want to know exactly how the sponsorship money will be spent. To this end, make sure you have a solid budget with appropriate quotes for the costs of the production and also be explicit if you have any other financial help or help in kind.

Sponsorship in kind

Sponsorship not only comes in the form of hard cash, it can also come in kind. Look at your production's needs and see if an appropriate company could supply goods that could be used as props or part of the stage set or costumes. A value will need to be attributed to the sponsorship in kind so you can fit it into your sponsorship packages. For smaller support, a pair of tickets and a quarter-page advertisement in the programme may be suitable.

Case study

Peterborough Mask Theatre

In 2002 and 2003, Peterborough Mask Theatre staged successive open-air productions of *Our Country's Good* and *A Midsummer Night's Dream* at Flag Fen Bronze Age Centre. The first year saw one major sponsor, but the following year they gained financial sponsorship from three significant sponsors, who covered all the production costs, even allowing radio advertising, and sponsorship in kind from a local printer (the full colour programme was designed and printed for free, which meant additional revenue came from advertisers) and a sound and lighting company who supplied technical equipment at a significantly reduced rate. The sponsors gained publicity through press and radio, regular press releases and interviews as well as having their own corporate night along with invited guests, where the director and other members of the society were available before the play and all the cast were present after the play to talk to the generous sponsors and guests. In effect, they didn't just take the money and run!

Grants

Other sources of funding may come from organizations such as the Arts Council or local authorities such as borough, county or town councils that may be able to contribute in the form of a grant. However, in all these cases, for a grant to be awarded the project has to be a new and special event. Government authorities are not going to give you money to stage *Oklahoma*!

National Lottery money is potentially available via the Arts Council through the Grants for the Arts and the Awards for All Scheme that does distribute grants of between £500 and

£10,000 to groups such as community theatre groups, with preference given to those with an annual income of less than £15,000. Look on the appropriate websites to find out about criteria, funds available and how to apply.

Useful addresses

UK: www.awardsforall.org.uk

England: www.artscouncil.org.uk

Northern Ireland: www.artscouncil-ni.org.uk

Scotland: www.scottisharts.org.uk

Wales: www.artswales.org

Advice can also be sought from organizations such as NODA, Arts and Business (Tel: 020 7407 7527), or the various national voluntary organizations.

UK: www.voluntaryarts.org (Voluntary Arts Network) Tel: 02920 395395

England: www.ncvo-vol.org.uk (National Council for Voluntary Organizations) Tel: 020 7713 6161

Northern Ireland: www.nicva.org (Northern Ireland Council for Voluntary Action)

Scotland: www.scvo.org.uk (Scottish Council for Voluntary Organizations)

Wales: www.wcva.org.uk (Wales Council for Voluntary Action)

The best approach

Initial contact with a potential sponsor or grant-awarding organization should be as personal as possible.

Identify the person you need to speak to within the company or organization. A simple phone call can achieve this.

The initial contact may take the form of a letter. Again make it personal and identify the person to whom the letter should be sent. Do not send generic or photocopied letters as this will be considered as junk mail and you know what you do with junk mail! The letter needs to be personal, concise and a selling document. Make clear who you are, what you are doing, why you need their support and the potential benefit to the organization (if a sponsor).

A telephone call to the right person again provides a personal touch, even if it is just a courtesy call to say you have sent a letter and would like, if possible, to talk further after they have received and read the letter. It could be an initial pitch to try and arrange a meeting.

If you can arrange a meeting with that person, do so. Take to the meeting everything you need in the way of information about the group, production, event and/or theatre and, very importantly, the facts and figures. You should be confident enough to answer any questions they may ask. Vague facts and figures are not helpful and do not impress; indeed, they can leave a negative impression which will not help your cause at all.

Remember, any meeting – and it may take more than one meeting to achieve your goal – shows that the company and/or organization is interested in the idea of being a sponsor or giving you a grant.

If you need to complete an application form for a grant from the Arts Council or local authority do talk to someone within the organization – and they will issue you with a contact name and number with your application pack – about the best way to fill in the application. They want to help you and it is best to ask if you're unsure about anything from the aptness of the application to a certain aspect of it.

Whatever the initial approach, always follow up what you have done. If you leave it after the first step you will have lost a potential source of funding. The fact is you have nothing to lose in applying for grants or seeking a sponsor. You will certainly be no worse off, while there is always the potential to gain.

'No' is not the end!

Do not take 'No' as a disaster or an affront. There are many reasons why your application may have been turned down, even when it seems like the perfect pitch. Try and find out why the application failed and keep a record of all the individuals, companies and organizations you have approached. Do not be put off re-applying to the same people and keep the communication lines open for there may be a benefit further along the line.

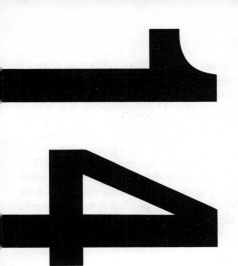

14
getting the ball rolling

In this chapter you will learn:
- how to find a play to perform
- how to apply for amateur rights and other licences
- what you can and can't do to a playscript
- about booking a venue.

Choosing a play

The first task for any theatre group is to select a play to perform. How theatre groups go about this can vary. Some groups have dedicated playscript readers who subsequently recommend plays to the committee. The committee is left then with the task of finding a director to direct a play. Other groups take recommendations from their membership and come to a decision after arranging a number of open play readings. A director may step forward with a play that they wish to do. The advantage here is that the director has usually done some homework already and has a good idea of how he/she would like to do the play. In effect, the director pitches a production to the committee for approval.

Amateur rights

Once you have a play that the group, approved by committee, wants to perform, the next step is to see if amateur rights are available. This can be done by enquiring of the company responsible for the amateur rights of the playscripts. In Britain, the organization that handles the amateur rights for the vast majority of plays is Samuel French Ltd. There are other companies that also handle amateur rights, but Samuel French Ltd is probably the main player.

A simple telephone call, email or written enquiry will enable them to tell you whether amateur rights are available. Unfortunately, there are occasions when amateur rights are temporarily withdrawn so that theatre groups are unable, for a time, to stage that production. There are a number of reasons why this may happen, with the often-cited professional touring production being one of them. It is still felt that an amateur production – which has to be marked as such on all publicity – can have a detrimental effect on the box office of a professional production. This, I believe, was designed to keep community theatre groups in their place and implies that the public who go to theatre are not very bright! Of course, the logical extension is that it is a compliment to community theatre that it can challenge the stars and budgets of the professional stage.

In addition to this, some plays may never have been available in the first place. The fact that a script is published does not mean that it may be performed. *The Mousetrap*, according to Paul

Taylor at Samuel French Ltd, is a classic example, as the publisher published the play over 50 years ago but it has never been released for amateur performance in this country!

Applying for a licence

If amateur rights are available then the next step is to apply for a licence. This is not a complicated business. All is required when applying is:

- the name of your theatre group
- the title of the play you're applying for a licence for
- the number of performances that will be staged
- the proposed venue and audience capacity
- the proposed dates of performance.

Plays are under copyright for 70 years after the playwright's death and permission always has to be sought (and usually paid for). Even if the production is for charity or educational purposes, or if only an excerpt is used for performance, a licence is needed. Indeed, even if there is no paying audience, permission has to be sought and a licence fee usually has to be paid. Remember, the licence fee that is paid is the only source of income the playwright receives from amateur productions.

Apply early

Planning is all-important, so make sure the performance licence is applied for well in advance. There have been occasions when amateur groups have left their application very late and then discovered that the amateur rights for their particular play were not available. With the theatre booked, publicity issued and rehearsals well under way it can be a devastating financial loss.

'On one occasion we were in the latter stages of the rehearsal of a play when we learned that the amateur rights were not available and we couldn't do it. We'd applied for the licence too late. Luckily we had another play in place to fill the theatre slot.'

Rich Unwin, Peterborough Mask Theatre

'We always advise groups to obtain their licences as far in advance as possible. Once you have obtained a licence you are legally entitled to perform that play or musical even if it is subsequently revived professionally and we are asked to withdraw the rights. Anyone who has applied and paid for a licence can still produce that title as the licence is a legal document. If such a licence has not been obtained, however, we can refuse rights if the work is the subject of a professional revival.'

Paul Taylor, Performing Rights Director, Samuel French Ltd

Samuel French Ltd

Samuel French Ltd are publishers of acting editions of musicals and plays primarily for the amateur theatre. They handle the performing rights to those plays as well as plays published by others. They also publish and sell a wide range of theatre books.

'The first thing to be borne in mind when you have decided upon a play or musical is that it is available for performance. Do this before you do anything else, including booking rehearsal rooms. There may be a number of reasons why a work might not be available to amateur groups. If a new play is still running in the West End or is on tour, then amateur rights will not yet have been released. When older plays are revived professionally, the title may be withdrawn from amateur performance altogether or within a certain radius of London (in the case of a West End revival) or in various parts of the country that a touring production is visiting.

'If an unlicensed amateur production clashes with professional plans there can be serious consequences for the amateur group and the production will certainly have to be cancelled with all the disappointment and financial losses that this involves. The golden rule is therefore to establish that the work you wish to perform is available for you and obtain your performing licence at the earliest opportunity.'

Paul Taylor, Performing Rights Director, Samuel French Ltd

Changes to the script

Any editing or rewriting changes to the script also need to be approved by the playwright or his agents. More often than not the answer will be 'No'. If the writer wanted the play different from his finished script he would have written a different version. There is also the question of casting. On occasions theatre groups, due to their own limited acting resources, may wish, for example, to change the sex of a character so it is played by an actress rather than an actor. This is a fundamental change to the script and needs express permission from the writer or his/her agent or there can be potential legal consequences.

It is less likely to be an issue if the change applies to a walk-on role or minor character with a few lines, such as if a waiter, for example, becomes a waitress.

Case study

A PRODUCTION of a Samuel Beckett play due to open on the Fringe has been entirely overhauled after the playwright's estate threatened legal action.

The Beckett estate has fiercely enforced the strict interpretation of the playwright's works since he died in 1989.

Act Without Words, by USA/Glasgow Productions, has a 15-strong cast and crew including students and actors from the United States and Scotland.

The show was produced by Daniel Graupner, a student at the Glasgow's Royal Scottish Academy of Music and Drama.

However, the production planned to mix the movement of *Act Without Words I* with the dialogue of *Act Without Words II*. Both plays were written in the 1950s.

Not I, a 20-minute monologue in which the drama is centred on the actor's lips, was to use a modern spotlight instead of a torch.

The Beckett estate refused permission for the production.

After months of rehearsals, actors have had to relearn the plays from scratch.

'Our production was far away from the actual script. It was pretty freely adapted. It was taking ideas about the show and seeing what would happen if we did this,' said Mr Graupner. 'We have had to change the whole show around and do it the way Beckett wanted it to be done.'

The Scotsman, August 2004

Out-of-copyright plays

Some plays are, of course, out of copyright, such as the complete works of William Shakespeare, and no permission or licence fee is required. There are literally hundreds of productions of Shakespeare's plays by both amateur and professional companies in Britain each year. In the summer they are extremely popular outdoor events. Interestingly, you never hear of professional productions of Shakespeare complaining that there is an amateur one down the road!

New writing

There is also the issue of a new play that may have been written by a member of the society. In this case, make the arrangement explicit with the playwright. Are they going to be paid? Or have they given their play to the group to perform for free? And if the play is to be directed by someone else, also address the issues of script editing and casting with the playwright.

Consequences of performing without a licence

On occasions theatre groups do try to avoid paying for the licence and gaining written permission to perform a play. This is both stupid and selfish: if the playwright had not written the play then theatre groups would have nothing to perform. More importantly, for a theatre group to recoup the money they have paid out to stage the play they need an audience. To get an audience the production has to be publicized. The respective agents will be made aware of this. Samuel French Ltd certainly does regular internet searches to check on possible rogue productions. They have the power to shut down a rogue amateur production either before the curtain goes up or during the run or, more dramatically, during a show. A further consequence could be that the amateur group concerned will never be given permission to stage a copyrighted amateur production again.

Case study

NODA pantomimes – copyright infringements

It was just a few months ago that a package landed on the desk of NODA's Chief Executive, Mark Pemberton containing a copy of a script for *Mother Goose*, a DVD of the production and an anonymous note suggesting we compare its contents to one of NODA's John Morley scripts. Close inspection revealed that the script, credited to the society itself, was almost word for word the same as the Morley script. And our records showed the society (which was not affiliated to NODA) had not applied for a licence. Clearly there had been a breach of the Morley Estate's copyright, in respect of which NODA Limited earns a commission on royalties.

NODA's Honorary Solicitor wrote to the society demanding reimbursement for outstanding royalties, script sales, video licence and interest on late payment, plus legal fees...

NODA National News, Winter 2006

Other licences

It is also worth mentioning at this point that another licence may need to be sought. For example, a licence would be needed from the Performing Rights Society for any music that is used within a production.

Amateur rights are exclusively for the live stage performance. They do not allow for the production to be recorded on film or video. The fact is, film and television rights – which are what this will fall under – are invariably held by somebody else and, even if these rights have been allocated, permission still needs to be sought from the copyright owner and this is a time-consuming business and certainly won't be given retrospectively. There are video-making businesses that claim to have relevant licences from the Mechanical Copyright Protection Society (MCPS) that will allow them to film your show. They may have a MCPS licence but it does not apply to the filming of theatrical productions.

Performing Rights Society

The Performing Rights Society (PRS) collects royalty fees on behalf of music writers and publishers for any public performance in the UK. A public performance is any music played – either live or recorded – outside the home and, therefore, can apply to theatrical venues and theatrical performances.

There is a misconception that a venue which already has a PRS licence to play music in the auditorium will be covered for any music that features in the production. It will not. So any atmospheric music, radio music, music on CD, etc. that features in the play needs a licence. This, of course, does not apply to musicals where the licence issued also gives permission for the songs and music to be performed as the overall piece of work. Since a venue's PRS licence does not provide blanket cover for an amateur theatre production, such companies will need to apply for a licence, seek permission and pay the appropriate fee for using music in the any of the following contexts:

- music played as an overture, *entr'acte* (interval) or exit music
- any incidental music, played live or recorded, during a play
- interpolated music – music not specially written for a particular theatrical production but performed by any number of characters to be heard by other characters in that production
- any songs that are not dramatically portrayed, e.g. 'Songs from the Shows'.

A PRS licence is not required for the performance of musicals, operas and operettas where the 'Grand Rights' have already been issued by the rights holders. Excerpts from musicals don't need a PRS licence if they are dramatically performed. Also, any music specifically written for a particular play or pantomime does not need a PRS licence.

With any performance licence it is best to apply as early as possible, and with the case of interpolated music PRS recommends applications should be made at least 30 days before the performance. You must have the appropriate licence in place or the performance either cannot take place or must take place without the unlicensed music.

It is normally permissible to perform excerpts from musical plays with a licence from the PRS provided that:

- the excerpt does not exceed 25 minutes duration
- it is not a complete act of the musical play

- it does not constitute a 'potted version' of the musical play
- it is performed without any change to either music or lyrics
- it is performed using only published or authorized musical arrangements
- there is no use made of any form of scenery, costume, choreography, staging, character representation or special lighting which gives a visual impression or other portrayal of the writer's original conception of the work from which it is taken.

In many cases, theatres, halls and other venues may have a blanket licence from the PRS (a licence to perform its entire repertoire). This should be ascertained beforehand and, in the absence of such a licence, application should be made to the PRS. It must be understood that royalties are payable to the PRS on all copyright music performed in a concert format.

Phonographic Performance Limited

Phonographic Performance Limited (PPL) is the UK record industry's collector of fees on behalf of record companies and performers. Their job is licensing the public performance and broadcasting of sound recordings. As such, a PPL licence will be required in addition to a PRS licence. Amateur operatic and dramatic societies are charged a special flat-rate tariff for background music used during the entry/exit of the audience, the intervals and during the performance.

Adaptations

It is also worth noting that adapting any other copyrighted work – such as a book, film, TV show, radio play, etc. – for the stage needs the express permission of the original authors or their agents. There may be a fee involved and restrictions imposed or there may simply be a 'No'.

The venue

Once amateur rights for the play have been confirmed and secured, the next step is to book a venue. Never enter into a written agreement (i.e. a contract) with a venue until amateur rights have been secured. Make the venue aware of the play you want to do because theatre managers need to know the nature of their season and avoid clashes within their own theatre and nearby venues. They will also want to avoid too many similar plays, particularly if they have to deal with several amateur groups or if a venue is open to both professional and amateur companies.

The venue will need to be assured that amateur rights have been secured before issuing a contract. Remember, you don't have a performance slot until the contract is signed. Theatre managers plan their programme well in advance, so community groups need to have their permission secured a minimum of six months before staging the production.

Community groups that own and run their own venue have this as an on-going process. They could be staging around a dozen productions of their own every year, so it is a big administrative job. A community drama group that performs in its local village hall probably has more time, but it is still recommended to secure the relevant permissions as early as possible.

Make sure that everyone knows what the conditions of the venue's contract are. There may be financial implications, for example, if a technical or dress rehearsal goes beyond a certain time or if the set isn't struck (that is, taken down) and the company have not vacated the venue by a given time. This is why community groups always ask (or rightly demand) that everyone helps with the get-out. Remember, any unnecessary financial costs on the current production will have an effect on the next production.

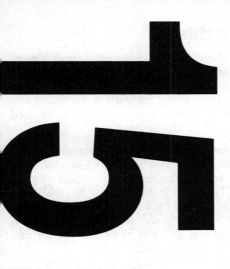

15

making the play happen

In this chapter you will learn:
- how to find actors
- what has to be done to stage a play
- how to publicize your play.

Auditions and casting

You have the play, the venue, the dates and number of performances booked. Now it is about making the play happen and the first stage of that is casting. Casting is achieved through auditions. Actors will put themselves forward for a particular role or roles and audition before the director and some trusted assistants. But where do you find the actors?

The first obvious choice is from within your own membership. If all the roles cannot be cast you may choose to hold an open audition which will allow actors who are not members of your theatre group to audition. The open auditions may be publicized through the local media, online and by any theatre publications. However, if a non-member is offered a role it must be a condition that they join the theatre group and pay the subscription and other costs (if applicable) before rehearsals begin.

Actors will be asked to perform an audition piece that is taken from the play. Initially it will be on this performance that the actor may or may not be cast. He/she may be required to audition again if competition is fierce for a particular role. However, the director has many factors to consider including a balanced cast. A musical analogy here is helpful. Eric Clapton is one of the best guitarists in the world but a band of Claptons, despite the abundance of talent, would be limited without other musicians playing other instruments such as drums or keyboards. Different skills are needed for different roles and this is particularly applicable in theatre. Leading actor A may be the best thing ever but if he doesn't look right or play with leading actress B, also fantastic, well then the play won't work. Failure at audition could be due to any number of reasons and should not prevent you treading the boards in the next production.

At the audition stage it is important to make clear what is expected of the actors who are cast, what the commitment will be and get them to indicate when they would be unavailable. After casting and armed with this information the next stage is rehearsals.

Rehearsals

Based on the information given at the auditions a rehearsal schedule will be drawn up to accommodate absence. The harsh fact is people do have work and holiday commitments but knowing what they are doing in advance will minimize the disruption to the rehearsal process. My own personal view is to never cast anyone who will be away in the week before the production or who could potentially miss a quarter of the rehearsals. Getting people to read in the part during rehearsal is never helpful to anyone least of all the absent actor or his fellow cast members. The vast majority of amateur productions do not have understudies so it is vitally important that everyone who is cast turns up when they should.

Rehearsal periods can vary. Some community groups rehearse two or three days a week with an increased and intense rehearsal period over the final two weeks. Others, particularly those who own their theatres, can have two or three productions on-going at any one time and they rehearse intensely over a month before curtain-up.

Often most community groups don't see the set or costumes until very late in the rehearsal process. Some companies don't even see and use the set until the get-in at the technical/dress rehearsal.

Technical rehearsal

From an acting point of view, technical rehearsals are a necessary evil of theatre. From a theatrical point of view they are an absolute must. They are invariably long and tedious to do. It is the moment when special effects of light and sound are introduced to the production to see whether they work and there are the practicalities of getting actors, scenery and props on and off stage. For the actors there are a lot of entrances and exits to walk through and plotting their position on stage in relation to the lighting. For everyone else it is to see whether the production works visually and audibly. The outcome of 'the tech' will set in stone the production you will put before your audience. Final decisions will have to be made quickly by the director and his creative team led by the stage manager, who will record diligently everything in the 'book' to make sure it will happen on the night. It is also here when Plan Bs are hatched. Namely, if something happens that shouldn't how will the actors or technical crew overcome it, hopefully, without anyone noticing? Guns on stage, for example, are notorious for jamming so if the gun fails to go off you need to think of an alternative quick death for the victim!

Dress rehearsal

The dress rehearsal – and, if you can, have more than one – is when everything comes together for the first (and possibly the last) time before performance. The play is run uninterrupted with all its foibles and *faux pas*! There is a mystic belief that a bad dress rehearsal will lead to a good opening night. While that may be true you do not consciously want to make a dress rehearsal a poor performance. If nothing else, a good dress rehearsal when everything comes together is a great boost to everyone who has been involved in the project that they really have a damn good play to perform before a live audience.

Publicity

Before that opening night you will have needed to arouse interest in the production and hopefully sold a few advance tickets. Advance tickets are another great boost because the cast and crew know that they have an audience. Without the audience, theatre – not just community theatre – cannot exist. So you need to tell everyone that the play is going to take place and encourage people to come along.

Posters and handbills

The first ports of call are posters and handbills. Poster design is very important and having a strong eye-catching image is vital. Remember where your posters and handbills are distributed and put up. Invariably they will be in theatres, libraries, offices, leisure centres etc. Places where there are lots of people and where there is myriad of literature and images all trying to entice those very same people to other attractions and interests instead of your play.

On those posters you want basic information that can be easily read, namely,

- name of drama or musical group
- title of play and playwright
- venue, dates and times of performance
- contact details for tickets.

The handbills should be mini versions of the poster but on the back of the handbills you can have a little précis of the play. Treat this as a pitch and make the play/musical sound as attractive as possible. Musicals have an advantage here because they can list the hit songs that everyone knows to lure musical lovers into the theatre. Further information about ticket prices and the various concessionary deals should be listed here.

If it is an open air production it would be wise to advise people about taking warm clothing and in what circumstances the production would be called off and make clear the policy about refunds.

Make it clear it's a community theatre production

On all printed publicity material you will be legally obliged as a condition of your performance licence to include the word 'amateur' to make clear it is a community theatre production and not a professional one. The name of the theatre group may have the word amateur in it such as Loughton Amateur Dramatic Society and so it is clear to the public it is a community theatre production.

If the word amateur does not appear in your group's name then a tag line is required, either a simple 'This is an amateur production' or to make a selling point of it with a tag line reading 'from the city's premier amateur group' or 'from the award-winning amateur theatre group' or 'the critically acclaimed amateur theatre group' etc. However, you must remember that any statement about your group and its production you make on your publicity has to be true and to make anything up could lead you into trouble.

Press publicity

Once the official production literature has been distributed – and utilize the membership to do this – other sources of publicity need to kick in. Press publicity is important in all its forms – not just the local newspaper press but also be aware of local magazines. Like the posters, have a strong photographic image you can distribute with your press releases. It does not need to be a picture from the scene of the play; look at your cast and see where the strongest image can be conjured up.

Press releases need to be informative – so make sure you put in all the basic details of the production – and attractive as a story in themselves. The harsh fact is that newspapers do not need to use your press release. On the scale of newsworthiness a play being staged by a local community theatre group is not a major story. At best it will be a paragraph tucked away on page 12 where readers will just glance over it.

Make your story of human interest. Look at your members and see if they have story – which they would be willing to share – that can help promote the play. A cast member may be making his 100th stage appearance with the group or been serving the group for 40 years. Alternatively, in real life your may have an actor who is a policeman by day but who is bringing his detecting skills as the Inspector in *An Inspector Calls*. Your group may be the first to stage an amateur production of a new West End play, or the group may have won an award for a recent production.

Another wave of press publicity can come from events that occur during the rehearsal process. I was involved with one production whereby one of our young actors, after weeks of fight choreography, ended up injuring his knee during a dance exam! In another production a young actor gained a place at Paul McCartney's Liverpool Institute of Performing Arts. These are human stories that newspapers love.

Newspapers and the public also like animal stories, for example, publicity may be generated from holding dog auditions for the musical *Annie*. Or have publicity photographs involving animals. For their production of *Animal Farm*, Peterborough Mask Theatre went to a farm to have their costumed actors photographed alongside the real animals they were suppose to be playing!

Deadlines

When planning this raft of publicity be aware of all the various media's deadlines. Look at the dates of your production and tie it into the various magazines publishing dates. Remember monthly magazines are invariably published the end of the previous month with an editorial deadline early that same month. Some magazines have deadlines of three months prior to publication. Contact the editors and find out what their deadlines are.

Advertising

Newspaper advertising is a vexed question. It is invariably expensive and you have to be sure the money you have spent and more can be recouped through ticket sales. It may be worth doing a survey of your patrons over the week of the performance and find out how they heard about the production so, in the future, you can spend your publicity money wisely.

Radio and TV publicity

Radio and, if you're very lucky, television interviews are a great way to gain publicity for your production as broadcasters reach far more people. Most areas of Britain have at least two local radio stations covering them – one from the BBC and the other a commercial station. If you do get an interview slot then send an interviewee who knows about the company, the play and will enthusiastically sell the production to the listeners. Do not send anyone who is dull of voice or anyone who just gabbles incoherently. Actors are good with scripted lines but can be useless as real people! With the BBC find out who is the local arts correspondent. Indeed, it is a good policy to find out who all the local arts and theatre writers are in your area and invite them along to the first night. The more reviews the better.

Radio advertising is another option. It can be expensive but commercial stations do repeat their ads frequently over a two-week or four-week period and so it will be heard. Again you have to find out if the financial investment was justifiable in terms of ticket sales.

Other publications and websites

Another area of publicity is the group's own website as well excellent websites such as **www.amdram.co.uk** or local theatre publications such as *Combinations* in Cambridge. Both feature publicity and post-production reviews of plays among the amateur theatre community.

Reviews

Reviews of your play can be good, bad, mixed or indifferent. Remember each review is one person's viewpoint although that viewpoint can be influential. On local newspapers reviews can be written by any one of a number of reporters and if you're lucky you may get a theatre-goer. Irrespective of their status, all reviews are legitimate providing the views expressed are the genuine belief of the reviewer.

Contact the reviewers of your local press, radio, websites and magazines and make sure they attend, are looked after and look out for their review. If a NODA member invites their Regional Rep to a performance, they will get a report in the regional magazine. Similarly there are other community theatre-specific magazines such as *Connections* in East Anglia that will also provide a review. These will appear long after the production has finished but they should still be welcomed and utilized. If a production is entered into a festival the Adjudicator's Report may also prove another welcome document.

Positive reviews are an asset and so it could be worthwhile to request a reproduction from the relevant reviewer for the website and anything good written about the group could be used for any future publicity. It would certainly support any tag line that boasts the group is 'critically-acclaimed'.

Most community theatre productions have week-long runs and so the effect of the local newspaper review may not be as influential anymore. However, a good review can certainly top up the Friday and/or Saturday audience but a negative one usually doesn't have people handing in their tickets and demanding a refund before curtain-up.

Word of mouth is still the best form of publicity. It is people coming along and seeing the production and then telling their friends about it and the group that will generate interest.

part three

other societies and legal requirements

16

community theatre production companies and theatre-owning societies

In this chapter you will learn:
- about community theatre production companies
- how to run your own theatre
- how the production process may differ in theatre-owning groups
- what problems may be encountered running your own theatre.

Community theatre production companies

Community theatre production companies differ from conventional community theatre groups in the way they are run and how they elect their committee.

Case study

Combined Actors of Cambridge

Combined Amateurs was initially set up by a group of actors who all contributed one pound to get the first production – *Man Alive* directed by Jim Railton – off the ground in 1965. Since then they have evolved into what is, in effect, an amateur production company called the Combined Actors of Cambridge (CAC). They stage three major productions, a festival and a touring production almost every year. It is run by a committee, which meets every month, but, unlike other community theatre groups, it has no members.

An open AGM is held where anyone interested in theatre can attend. Being a member of the CAC committee, however, is no token position and the commitment expected of anyone joining Combined Actors is made clear from the outset.

'It is quite hard to ask somebody to be on a committee without saying to them "you will be expected to work hard; you won't be expected to just come to the meetings, you will be expected to do your bit,"' explained Julie Petrucci, Combined Actors' secretary for over 25 years.

Combined Actors, like any other committee, try to attract and retain younger actors but they recognize it is important to have some people with technical knowledge and some with an interest in backstage. Their knowledge is invaluable when helping directors with the actual practicalities of their production.

Without members, productions are generated from the amateur theatre community and Combined Actors welcome anyone with an idea for a future production. Directors are invited to pitch their ideas, including performing rights availability and an application form for those rights, for a production to the committee. A reading committee exists to read the plays and they pass on their recommendations about the production to the main committee.

'We have an uneven number on that reading committee so that hopefully we get a majority,' explained Julie. 'But if they say "we hate it" then we may get the director in and say talk to us about it, tell us what your ideas are and that might alter the view because sometimes plays come off the page better. So once we have discussed things with the director we usually ask him either to go away or say we will discuss it and get back to him and very often that is the best way because it means then you can completely discuss whether it is going to be a viable option. And sometimes we can take a risk and do something that is reasonably obscure and we possibly think that might be an interesting thing to do. It would be a good piece of theatre. Would it get bums on seats? Maybe not. Could we afford to take the risk on it? Then maybe we would say we will take a risk on it but we will do it at a smaller venue and not hire a big theatre.'

The Combined Actors' committee – like any other society – carries a huge responsibility, not least to its own well-earned reputation.

'A few years ago we had a couple of directors come to us who were new to us, new to Cambridge. We said to them we would like you to do something for us but we can't go with a full-length production; would you like to do a smaller production or would you like to do a festival play? Just so that we can see how they are, and in that case the committee works quite a bit closer with the director than we would normally,' said Julie.

'We watch very carefully how they are with the cast because Combined Actors have a huge reputation. We have been going since 1965 so we know what we are about. We can't afford to alienate the actors who like to work with us by having a director who doesn't treat them well.

'Sometimes you get a director who loves to workshop them and talk through the text and some actors don't like doing that. Some actors hate to do workshops. One of them said to me, "there is a limit to how long I want to be a mushroom".

'Every director has his/her own system. Personally, I like to talk about the scripts and characterisation before we start rehearsal and then just leave them and let them find their own level and take it from there. If they are not doing anything with the character then you have to do the work. Usually people like to discuss how the director sees the character and put their own slant on it as well.

So, having a very new director who we are not familiar with is a risk. We have learned our lesson the hard way. We have also learned our lesson in putting on musical productions. We are not a musical group as such. We've had two or three stabs at doing the musical – all were a nightmare and all lost a huge amount of money. So really musicals aren't our thing; we leave those to the musical groups.'

If an idea is accepted then, in return, the committee will put together a production package including a venue, production budget, help, support and advice for the successful director.

A production manager from within the committee is allocated to the director, who has to attend all committee meetings during the tenure of the production. The director is responsible for putting together his/her own production team before auditions take place. Each member of the production team, particularly newcomers to CAC, must be approved by the committee before being confirmed in the post. A CAC production team will include stage manager, set co-ordinator (design, construction and painting), lighting designer, sound designer, properties manager, wardrobe supervisor, publicity and programme manager, front-of-house manager and production manager.

The Combined Actors have a long-standing association with the Penguin Club – a Cambridge-based autonomous group of technical and backstage crew with extensive local knowledge – from whom the stage manager should ideally be appointed.

Open auditions are held on all Combined Actors' productions. The director has to supply an outline of the production and character profiles (including age ranges). The open auditions are advertised in CAC's amateur drama monthly newsletter, *Combinations,* which is distributed widely in the Cambridgeshire region and beyond, with over 200 individual subscriptions and many group subscriptions. *Combinations* is utilized by many of the community theatre groups in the area to advertise their productions, auditions, festivals, help needed and other events, and carries reviews of some of the productions.

The director is solely responsible for casting and arranging rehearsals. All Combined Actors productions have a minimum of 20 rehearsal sessions of minimum two-hour duration over a two- to three-month period before the dress rehearsal. In addition, the director, aided by the production manager, organizes the necessary meetings with the production team.

There is a benefit to not having any members in that there is no obligation to include anyone. Actors are cast solely on their ability to do a given part with no one excluded. Julie recalls: 'The nice thing is, and I can't remember the last time it hasn't happen, you always get new people. It is really lovely having new people in the cast working with people who are experienced working with the company. The established people know our reputation and so the others get the kudos of being in this group. To get on the stage at the ADC Theatre or at a theatre that has a big following as far as audience goes is good.'

Actors are required to pay subscriptions and for scripts in relation to the production in which they are involved.

However, being a production company without any roots that performs in many different theatres can be an issue, not only in terms of performance venues but rehearsal venues as well. Village-hall and theatre-owning societies certainly have an advantage in this respect over societies such as Combined Actors and BAWDS (another Cambridge-based amateur production company). Luckily, CAC has attracted a solid core audience which supports their efforts.

'We have quite a big audience following and I think over the years the line between amateur and professional, as far as Combined Actors is concerned, has slightly blurred. People aren't quite sure whether we're professional or not because the productions are always very good,' said Julie.

'Whatever the company, the bottom line is: Does the audience want to see this play? To be perfectly honest, if there was a play I was keen to see I wouldn't mind who was doing it. I'd mind afterwards if it was done badly if I'd paid good money.

'People, in this area who are a bit snooty about amateur theatre don't appreciate the quality of the productions. I'm talking from experience. I go round reviewing for the magazine. I go round all sorts of places and sometimes I'm quite stunned at the professionalism of people who do it in this little tiny place they've built a stage on and they only have one way to get on to the stage. People are so inventive and I think that in the main they are very proud of being able to put on what they consider to be a good production – and the majority of them are.

'Sometimes you go to village groups that are run by people who have always run them. This is how they've always done them and this is the way they will always do it. They still work on the premise they can get away with murder, but the news to them is they can't, not these days. People are much, much more perceptive than they used to be.

'You do come in for criticism and you are at risk if you don't put on a good production or you don't give it your all – people won't go next time and they'll say "Oh no, I remember when we went to see so-and-so there, do you remember that chap who...", you know.

'You also have to be careful with your casting; in our group we also say you've got to field your best cast.'

Theatre-owning societies

Many community theatre groups dream of owning and running their own theatre. A fortunate few are lucky enough to do just that. There is enormous benefit to doing so, not least artistically, when you can perform a regular season of plays. On average most theatre-owning groups can stage around eight productions a year, possibly more if they have a youth theatre or an additional studio theatre as a performing space.

It sounds attractive but it does make demands on the membership, particularly the much sought after backstage technical crew. The fact is, the number of productions is dictated by the necessity to generate income to pay for the upkeep and maintenance of the theatre that is invariably run by unpaid volunteers, namely, its members.

The Little Theatre Guild

The Little Theatre Guild (LTG) was founded in 1946 with nine original members. It now boasts approximately 100 independently controlled amateur-run theatres. In addition there are a host of other amateur-owned or volunteer run theatres that are not members of the LTG.

To be a member of the LTG the society must be independent and self-governing and own or control its theatre building and be responsible for the upkeep and maintenance. The theatre must be 'non-commercial in character', that is, it is not run for profit for the benefit of shareholders or the like. Regular productions must also run at the venue.

There is tremendous advantage to running your own venue, not least of which is running your own season and choice of plays. Certainly the volunteer-run Norbury Theatre in Droitwich could host Studley Operatic Society's production of *Show Boat* after it had been banned from the Redditch Council-owned Palace Theatre over the 'blacking up' controversy (see Chapter 17).

However, owning and running your own theatre is not all about the plays and musicals you are staging. The theatre building needs as much, if not more, love and care as the productions on stage. The fact is, performing arts buildings vary in design and age and face different problems. They can be large opera-type venues or small experimental drama spaces. Indeed, many of the LTG member theatres boast both a main auditorium and a studio theatre in buildings that were not originally designed as theatres but have been converted into one.

Generally speaking, main auditoria are preserved while improvements and upgrades are made to technical equipment, front-of-house facilities like foyers and back-of-house facilities such as dressing rooms. Many improvements may be forced upon the society by legislation, for example, child protection issues necessitate a separate dressing room for children. There may be a need to accommodate access for the disabled like installing lifts or widening seating areas.

Technical equipment for lighting and sound has improved enormously in recent years and any self-respecting theatre wants the best available for both the members and the audience. However, there may be limitations, particularly on older buildings, as to whether such advanced and often complex lighting and cabling would be suitable.

Case study: theatre maintenance and improvements

Below are real-life examples of the kind of work theatre-owning companies need to undertake to maintain or upgrade their buildings.

Royalty Theatre

In the late 1980s and early 1990s the non-professional Royalty Theatre in Sunderland embarked on a series of improvements that any theatre is likely to face at some point.

- A new bar was installed and their Green Room was refurbished, while £30,000 was paid to cure dry rot.
- The exterior of the theatre was redecorated and illuminated signage was added.
- The refurbished dressing rooms had new carpets, as did the rehearsal rooms.
- The main auditorium (216 capacity) was given new flooring, seats and carpet.
- The proscenium arch was enlarged. The 60-seater studio theatre was redecorated and new drapes, plinths and chairs were added.
- The main lighting stock was upgraded and a new computerized stage lighting control was installed.

Medway Little Theatre

More recently, the Medway Little Theatre in Rochester, Kent, a relative newcomer to the LTG, had to remove six audience seats to comply with health and safety regulations on access. They installed a new and expensive but very necessary fire alarm system, redecorated and refurbished their main auditorium (100-seat capacity) and rehearsal room and acquired a set of second-hand seating from the National Theatre in Northampton.

Theatr Fach

Theatr Fach (Dolgellau Amateur Dramatic Society) successfully applied for a National Lottery grant to add an extension to their existing building to create more space for backstage facilities and a clubroom.

Practical considerations of owning a theatre

Maintenance

One of the biggest problems facing amateur-run theatres is maintenance. Often, financial constraints can mean expensive reactive maintenance. A problem is put off because the money isn't there and then the problem becomes worse and there is no option left but to deal with it. Ideally, regular on-going maintenance is the key where problems are identified and can be dealt with as early as possible.

Any major work would necessitate closing the theatre, but when a theatre is dark it is not generating the income it needs to pay for such things.

Energy bills

Another major cost for theatres is energy bills, particularly for electricity which, as for everyone else, is subject to a fluctuating energy market. A series of special effect lighting productions can also have an adverse effect on the electricity bill. There are also gas and water bills to consider.

Income

The main source of income is the box office, so a decision has to be made about a programme that, by necessity, has to get bums on seats. Smaller studio theatres provide an opportunity to experiment and try out new directors but still provide a smaller source of income. Membership subscriptions, donations from the public, a licensed bar, sponsorship and funding for specific projects can all bring the much-needed cash not only to keep your theatre group going but also its prized theatre. The theatre, too, could be hired out to other amateur, professional or other groups.

Case study

Leicester Little Theatre

Leicester Little Theatre is owned and run by Leicester Drama Society (LDS). It boasts a 349-seat main auditorium and the 60-seat Hayward Studio. They stage at least 12 main productions a year plus a highly entertaining and money-spinning pantomime.

Leicester Drama Society, according to John Graham's interesting book *Before My Time*, was formed back in 1922 and became resident in the Leicester Little Theatre in 1930, before becoming owners in 1932. The building was originally a 19th-century Baptist Chapel that was acquired by the Independent Order of Rechabites in 1919. The Independent of Rechabites was a friendly society that eventually evolved into a financial institution. They were part of the temperance movement and were fundamentally opposed to the consumption of alcohol on both moral and health grounds.

Despite disputes between landlord and tenants, the Order proved a good ally for Leicester Drama Society, not only selling them the building that was to become the Leicester Little Theatre but also arranging loans to help with the maintenance and development of the society. The last of the monies from the Rechabite loans was paid off in the mid-1960s when the LDS made the economic decision to open a bar in February 1966 which, due to their association with Rechabites, they had been previously unable to do.

In April 1955 a fire ripped through the building, necessitating significant improvements and refurbishment. Since then the society has gone from strength to strength and acquired more property so that the theatre boasts rehearsal rooms, costume hire shop, scenery storage and workshop.

Leicester Drama Society's season comprises at least 12 productions each year in its main theatre. This places production demands on both actors and crew. An actor cast in a Leicester Drama Society production can expect an intense rehearsal period lasting approximately six weeks which requires the actor to commit to attending and participating in many evening weekday rehearsals. (This is common practice in many amateur-run theatre societies.)

Most productions run for one week, but at any one time Leicester Drama Society has at least three shows in various stages of production. This is not just the situation for the cast but also all those involved in costume, props, set design and building, marketing, etc.

'We have two shows in rehearsal – one in later stages of rehearsal, one in earlier stages of rehearsal – one in audition stage and even one on stage. It is a conveyor belt,' explained LDS secretary John Ghent.

This programme – which is both artistically and financially necessary for the group to fulfil their legal obligations as well as maintain and continually improve the theatre – is demanding on the membership.

Leicester Drama Society holds regular open days/evenings that allow the public to see behind the scenes at the theatre while meeting many of the members already involved. These open days are a source of recruitment for both onstage and offstage talent as well as a marketing tool to attract new audience members.

Actors can audition on a production-by-production basis or, alternatively, LDS holds a general audition at which actors perform audition pieces of their own choice. The benefit of this is that the actors are placed on an actors' register, which can be used by directors as a resource to cast LDS productions.

There is also a demand on the group's existing directors. New and experienced directors are always being sought. LDS will try to see the work of an experienced director before he is added to the directors' list, while a new director, partnered with an appropriate mentor, could be offered the opportunity to direct a production in the 60-seater Haywood Studio. Success and experience gained there can lead to a new director getting his/her production staged in the main theatre.

One benefit of owning your own theatre is that, in all probability, you will own your technical equipment such as lights and sound systems. With that comes your own in-house technician who will offer to mentor anyone interested in either of these disciplines and are also sufficiently open-minded to welcome input from experienced lighting and sound personnel. It is fair to say that technicians, because there are too few of them, are in more demand and almost have to staff every show. The influx of new blood is welcome but the existing team will want to be absolutely sure new recruits are ready before taking the helm at one of the shows.

Leicester Drama Society also does regular standalone workshops that cover subjects such as acting, stage management, sound, lighting, make-up and so on, aimed at newcomers and experienced members.

Costume is another area of vital importance to the theatre. With so many shows staged by LDS the costume department is always busy and has stored up an impressive catalogue of costumes. LDS's costume department works as a separate business, hiring out costumes not only to other amateur societies but for parties as well. It has become a vital income stream.

In recent years the LDS has resurrected its own Youth Theatre, with junior and senior sections, which has proved very popular. Apart from encouraging youngsters to get involved it could potentially provide a conveyor belt to the LDS adult productions. The Youth Theatre is producing financially successful productions too.

Like professional theatre, the most important production in terms of income has become the annual pantomime, which has a longer run and attracts near capacity audiences every year.

The Leicester Little Theatre also hires the venue to other amateur groups and books one-off standalone professional shows such as musical hits or 'an audience with' type shows. It also hosts its own speech and drama festival.

Such a theatre has, of course, obligations of both a legal and a financial nature. Leicester Little Theatre, like many theatres, is an old building and needs constant maintenance and improvements as the law and the paying public dictate. There is also a need to employ professionals and staff on occasions.

'Health and safety officials said our staircase was not deemed wide enough so we had to build a new staircase, the consequence of which was a reduced-size men's dressing room. Some of the musical societies can get a bit crammed.

'We also have members who are good at heating and plumbing, etc. and we sort of use them where we can,' said John Ghent.

LDS produces a monthly newsletter called *Scene* that keeps the members up to date with events but also lists the up and coming productions, with audition details.

Christine Hewson is Leicester Little Theatre's LTG representative and is a long-serving Leicester Drama Society committee member, performer and director. She explained how the society is run.

'We have a Board of Trustees that is elected by the membership. They have a shelf life in the first instance of two terms of three years, then each term is three years. When we first set up those terms were staggered: some served one, some two and some three so they weren't going *en masse*. From the membership, teams were elected for productions and facilities. People are nominated for a team and voted for. Very often we don't get to a vote because not enough people are interested or able to give the time.'

The committee constitutes a chairman, honorary secretary, company secretary (who is not a trustee) and then members responsible for facilities, productions and marketing (all of whom head up teams). The remaining two members of the committee are without portfolio. Meetings are held on Sunday mornings.

The production team begins planning in August of their first year of office for the programme that will start in September the following year. Christine Hewson explained:

'Productions teams have a shelf life of two years. First year they are production planning, second year they look after the programme they have planned while a new production team begins planning. They overlap. Everything used to be done by one production team but that is really hard work.

'They have to think about what plays will be contained in a season. They write to directors to give them three choices and ask if they are prepared to direct any of those things – there is no guarantee they will be chosen but proposals will be read and discussed. They also ask the audience and membership for suggestions. They also look at new stuff that has been released.'

The only rule to which the season planners have to adhere is to put two named authors at the start of each half of the season and the audiences will invariably come.

'We know our audience. People say we have to do such-and-such to attract a new audience but there is no such thing as a new audience. The audience you get at this theatre – people say your audience will die off and there won't be anybody left – but this theatre has been going for 80-odd years with the same kind of audience.

'You may attract more people, extra people and some of the plays will attract a different kind of person but you won't ever attract, in my experience and knowing of other places, people who come to theatre who have got a lot of family commitments or whose kids haven't grown up with theatre. What we've got here is a very healthy nucleus who, whenever our new brochure goes out, immediately book six plays for the price of five, or five plays for four. The audience is always the same kind of people.'

There are problems of maintenance and membership that have to be addressed, and being part of the LTG has helped LDS deal with those issues.

'Building costs and keeping up with new regulations like Health & Safety have been a nightmare over the last few years. You really have to educate yourself to risk assessments, their consequences and solutions. Meeting with different theatres under LTG is very useful.

'Casting and backstage people are a problem – again not enough personnel. And sometimes finding directors for plays is difficult. There are some directors we don't rate very highly so you wouldn't go towards them unless you absolutely had to.

'Some directors are far too incestuous to a degree. There are some who don't look anywhere except under their noses. Comfort-zone directors are not the most apt people to have in charge of a production and in the worst cases it can show on the stage.'

Case study

Kings Theatre

Kings Theatre is a 123-seat capacity venue owned and run by Newmarket Operatic, Musical and Dramatic Society (NOMADS). NOMADS stage around eight productions a year as well as running a youth group. They hire the venue out to both amateur and professional companies. They have a licensed bar and a wardrobe department that hires out costumes to other groups. In 2007 they finally became a registered charity.

In 1955 NOMADS Chairman, Captain H. R. King, bought Fitzroy Rooms, a restaurant that was originally St Mary's Church of England School. He bequeathed it to NOMADS after his death. The conversion into a theatre was successfully undertaken by the group and is now a modern-equipped theatre. NOMADS' elected committee from its 120+ membership runs the Kings Theatre, which is held in trust by three trustees. In addition to the amateur and professional shows staged at the theatre, the venue is hired for other entertainments and activities.

NOMADS also boasts a 50+ strong Young NOMADS group for 8- to 18-year-olds. To join the youth group, young people must attend the annual audition (to fill vacancies created when members have left) before the youth leader, assistant youth leader and a committee made up of Young NOMAD members. The success of the Young NOMADS has brought financial benefits that have been converted into equipment and improved décor for the theatre and NOMADS as a whole.

NOMADS also offers a costume hire service from their theatre wardrobe department for certain musical and pantomime costume sets or individual costumes.

The theatre recently established itself as a limited company with a charitable status, ostensibly so that it is able to raise funds in a more formalized way and make NOMADS a better organization. At one stage NOMADS had a rather unwieldy 18-strong committee.

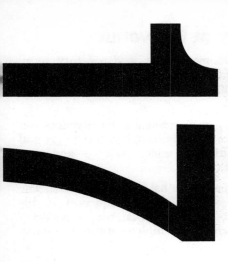

17

safety and other legal requirements

In this chapter you will learn:
- how to create and implement a health and safety policy
- how to create and implement a child protection policy
- how the Data Protection Act affects group and audience members
- how to create and implement a disciplinary and grievance procedure
- how the Licensing Act affects theatre performances where alcohol is sold
- about issues relating to the portrayal of race.

Health and safety at the venue

Health and safety has become almost a derogatory term, particularly in the world of theatre where it is often associated with expensive and costly building work. Unfortunately, it is the law and we have to comply.

The first task is to carry out a risk assessment of the venues you use – established theatres will already have had one so get and read a copy of their health and safety policy – and then undertake the recommendations.

Most health and safety measures are basic common sense. The question to ask is: What will be the consequences if this happens? The second question is: What we can reasonably do to prevent this happening? Then simply implement the reasonable preventative measures.

It is important to appoint a health and safety officer for each production to ensure that the policy is implemented. That person – and indeed all members – needs to be familiar with the policy. Everyone needs to be made aware of who is responsible for maintaining and checking the safety of different aspects of the production and/or venue, ranging from what to do in the event of evacuation to dealing with on-stage pyrotechnics. If any problems do occur they need to be reported and the policy should be reviewed and revised accordingly.

It has to be remembered that we live in an increasingly litigious society and your group does not want to be sued by a member of the public or one of your own members because something that could reasonably have been prevented occurred, causing injury. It is not difficult to achieve, as even modest-sized community theatre groups have demonstrated.

Case study

Bramley Parish Theatre Players

Leeds-based Bramley Parish Theatre Players regularly perform at the local St Margaret's Church and have instigated a safety policy for that venue which they publish on their website. The policy is reviewed after each production and is updated annually.

In 2007 Bramley Parish Theatre Players staged a successful pantomime, *Puss In Boots*, with an established safety policy in place. After the production they carried out a review to see how successful it was and to identify any problems that needed to be addressed in the review.

Chairman Edward Turner explained how the Policy worked:

'Responsibility for implementing the health and safety policy lies with the whole group, who have access to copies. The stage manager has his own copy and is charged to follow and ensure the implementation of the policy on stage during performances and before and during rigging. The authority of the stage manager and his/her role in ensuring safety on stage is stressed to all the cast. Any on-stage dangerous incidents are recorded for action to prevent their recurrence. In any case the policy is reviewed annually following the pantomime.

'The whole cast and stage crew sign in and out. Those under 18 do not leave the building until collected by a responsible adult unless we have signed parental/carer authority to allow them to leave. This also applies to front-of-house helpers. On performance nights there is a printed list to make names easier to read in the event of an evacuation, as more people are present than at the average rehearsal. At the fire practice we found the signing-in book was difficult to read and would most likely have been impossible to read for the fire steward who may not know everyone by name.

'We have a fire steward who makes sure that any fire hazard during performance – e.g. flash pots – is carefully monitored. He/she also notes the position of any person of reduced mobility to be ready in case of evacuation. We have held two fire practices – the second of which was to assess whether the change of instructions on evacuation had overcome the problems encountered on the first. Thankfully they did. The fire steward holds a cast, crew and helpers list for evacuation purposes. During our preparation for the pantomime, we held two fire drills – the second because the first had highlighted some problems.

'The first aid team is obviously present at performances, but a designated first aider is always present at rehearsals, set-building and painting and rigging. During this year's performance on one night we actually had a relatively serious first aid incident requiring an ambulance that needed us to close one of the exits when the performance finished. This is recorded in the building's first aid ID book and ours.

'We use a building owned by others and our safety and fire drills have been of use in helping them amend their safety procedures for other hall users. We have the largest group – up to the fire safety limit – of people in the building and so are faced with more problems than those with 10–15 people present at meetings.'

Smoke and vapour effects

On occasion your production may use certain types of special effects that utilize smoke and vapour to create the effect, for example, dry ice, oil mist, glycol/mineral oil smoke or pyrotechnic smoke. Their use falls under the Control of Substances Hazardous to Health Regulations (1994). For all these effects the manufacturers, by law, must provide information about the potential hazards that may arise when using these products. These potential hazards must form part of any risk assessment carried out by the group or venue.

Community theatre groups need to be aware that smoke making does obscure visibility and so the potential for slips and trips is heightened, with the same potential problems occurring with spilt oil. Freeze burns, frostbite and skin irritation are all potential problems, while the most extreme is asphyxiation due to high concentrations of carbon dioxide or nitrogen gases. It is important to pay attention to the occupational exposure standards (OES) of each substance. Use that is below the OES should not constitute a problem, but asthmatics and smaller children may still be affected. Any risk identified must, by law, be eliminated or controlled so far as is reasonably practicable.

Any risk assessment needs to consider not only the operator and performers but also the audience. It is not possible to know the make-up of an audience let alone any who may have asthmatic problems or are elderly. Always err on the side of caution when using such smoke effects and be aware that they might obscure exits in case of an emergency.

Preventing exposure is the key, and a competent operator should be able to prevent or seriously limit exposure to audience and backstage crew. The operator in particular needs protecting with appropriate safety clothing and eye protection for the substance being used.

It is very important for the theatre group to forewarn the audience that such smoke effects (and certain lighting effects) are going to be used either on posters, tickets, written warning signs at the venue and a verbal announcement at the venue before the show starts.

Information sheets are available from: HSE Information Centre, Broad Lane, Sheffield S3 7HQ or the HSE infoline on 0845 345 0055.

Audience safety

The safety of the audience is paramount and is something all community theatre groups should be aware of as part of their risk assessment of the venue. Managing a crowd is probably at its height at just before curtain-up and after curtain-down, particularly in the latter case, when everyone is leaving the auditorium either for their cars in the car park or for a post-show drink in the bar. Recognize where there is the potential for bottlenecks and consider late arrivals, queues outside the women's toilet and queues for refreshments at the interval.

Invariably, it is the society's front-of-house team that has face-to-face contact with the audience. They are responsible for keeping the customers safe by keeping queuing to a minimum at a kiosk, for the toilet or at the box office – in fact, any static group of people may cause problems. Keeping people moving safely and comfortably is most important of all. An unpleasant experience through stress because of overcrowding can have a negative effect on your next production's box office.

Make sure everything is clearly signposted from auditoria, programme sellers, refreshment kiosks, bars, toilets, box office, car park. This is particularly important if the venue has undergone any refurbishment or layout changes. People go with the familiar even when the familiar is not there or has changed. Be aware of where you place your sponsor's stand or where your programme sellers are positioned. Make sure they do not contribute to crowd congestion.

Stage weaponry

The first and foremost question any community theatre group should ask is whether they really do need weapons in their production. If so (i.e. they are explicit in the script), what is the best way of handling them?

If any weapon is to be used – real or fake – in a production, permission must be sought from the police, who should be contacted and informed of the intended use of the weapons in relation to the script.

Security is of paramount importance when weapons are involved; whatever the weapon or weapons to be used for the production there will need to be strict security in place relating to its safe-keeping and handling. The best policy is to minimize the number of people who handle the weapon. It should be restricted to the actor or actors using it and the props supervisor or stage manager. Ideally, a person with no other production responsibilities should serve as the weapons supervisor. They will keep the weapon under lock and key. Furthermore, all weapons need to be stored in a secure area requiring two keys to access them. There should be a written plan of what happens to the weapon and who is responsible for it at any given time. This is particularly important for open-air productions.

On no account should any weapon be carried or used in a public area, including when characters walk down the aisle to the stage.

Any blade-type weapons must have their edges and points ground off to make them blunt.

Stage fighting

Any stage fighting – unarmed or armed – needs to be choreographed by a competent fight arranger. Due consideration must be given to the fitness and capabilities of the actors involved in the fight. A risk assessment will need to be carried out and any potential problems need to be identified and adequate precautions taken. The most important aspect of any stage fights is rehearsal supervised by an experienced fight arranger.

Stunts

Stunts on stage really need to be performed by a competent stunt person. If actors wish to undertake their own stunts then a stunt co-ordinator with relevant experience and training needs to be on hand to make sure the actors undertake those stunts safely. A risk assessment is required with identifiable risks minimized. Once again, due consideration must be given to the fitness and capabilities of the actor undertaking the stunt.

Smoking on stage

Under the Health Act 2006 it is now illegal to have actors smoking a cigarette, cigar or pipe on stage in Northern Ireland, Scotland and Wales. In England there is an exemption 'if the artistic integrity of the performance makes it appropriate'. In essence, an actor smoking on stage has to be integral to the plot and not just an accessory.

However, even if the actor can smoke on stage he/she will be unable to do so in the rehearsal room. Village halls, school halls or any public building where rehearsals take place will be designated no-smoking areas, so there is no opportunity to rehearse the act of smoking in the context of the character's moves and dialogue.

Current legislation means a £50 fine will be imposed on the offending actor if he lights up in rehearsal, but he will only be penalized on stage if his smoking is not deemed to be of 'artistic integrity'.

Child protection policy

Drama teacher John Owen was charged with sex offences against boys at a school in Wales. Owen, who committed suicide before going to court, was believed to use drama as a 'vehicle for improper activity with children' which constituted serious sexual abuse...

This case led to the Clywch Inquiry in 2004, which issued recommendations about the teaching of drama in school...

Sara Reid, the Welsh Assembly's assistant Children's Commissioner, said: 'The risk of someone being able to behave in an abusive or sexually abusive way towards young people is greater in drama.'

Source: *Western Mail*, 17 February 2006

Director of Harborough Youth Theatre, James Adkins, was found guilty of three counts of indecent assault... The court heard how he had abused his power as director and producer, picking mild-mannered victims who desperately wanted to be on stage.

Source: *The Stage*, 12 February 2005

Child protection is paramount in community theatre. The very nature of theatre is based on intimacy and absolute trust of all concerned. It is extremely important for any musical or drama group, particularly youth and school groups, to adopt a child protection policy and have procedures in place for dealing with suspicion or disclosure of abuse. Quite frankly it is not worth the risk for anyone to stick their head in the sand or complain of the additional costs in protecting children and vulnerable people. Although child sex abuse represents only 0.1 per cent of recorded crime, no one will want their society to be part of that statistic, especially if they have done nothing to prevent such a thing happening.

Any group that has children in its ranks or can reasonably expect to offer opportunities to children in the future needs to have a child protection policy and procedures for implementing it. NODA produces a model child protection policy that member and affiliate societies can adopt and, more importantly, implement.

If a drama group wants to become a registered charity then it will be required to have a written child protection policy approved by the Charity Commission. Every group – seeking charity status or not – should have a child protection policy and appropriate procedures of which all their members are aware. The policy will need to be updated and reviewed on a regular basis.

For any production or event in which children are involved, there needs to be a risk assessment and risk management. These will identify potential dangers/opportunities for an abuser in relation to how the society operates.

Publicity in print and online is now part and parcel of community theatre, but with regard to children there needs to be editorial prudence in terms of the types of photographs used and any information about the child performer. Sadly, computer technology can allow the manipulation of images, so due consideration should be given to the photographs used. In this respect, get parental approval and explain where the photographs will be published and displayed online.

By that same token, be very aware of editorial content regarding biographical information in programmes and online. The only biographical information that should ever be divulged is the name of the child actor. No other reference should be made to the child's school, clubs, interests, where they live or even who their parents are – people can be identified from what seems an insignificant amount of information.

One backstage policy that should exist is the banning of cameras or mobile phones with cameras, especially in dressing rooms.

Chaperones

Chaperones are the front-line soldiers in preventing and minimizing the opportunity for any form of abuse. The chaperone (and hence the group) is responsible for the child from the moment of arrival to the moment of departure when the child is picked up by his/her parents or guardian. One chaperone can be responsible for up to 12 of the same sex children and will be concerned with the children's conditions and well-being for the duration of the production. Any concerns the chaperone may have should be voiced to the producer/director. The child's welfare is paramount and if a chaperone deems a child to be too tired or ill then the chaperone's loyalty first and foremost is to the child and they should not allow them to continue.

CRB

The people who perform the role of chaperone need to be trusted, so to this end NODA recommends that community theatre groups need to have people checked through the Criminal Records Bureau (CRB) by an Enhanced Disclosure. An Enhanced Disclosure will reveal any convictions, cautions, reprimands and warnings held on the police computer. There is a fee involved and the application has to be taken by the individual concerned, and for which a certificate will be issued. If anyone has an existing disclosure certificate, make sure it is up to date, but you are recommended to ask the person to apply for a new certificate that is relevant to the society. In Scotland no disclosure is transferable between organizations.

It may be in the group's interest to get as many members as possible checked so that the chaperone role does not fall solely to one or two people each time. A parent can look after their own child but the same person will need to be CRB checked to look after any other children.

The information on CRB disclosures requires confidentiality and secure storage and, when necessary, disposal. When applying for disclosure the group will have to have a designated contact who will handle such matters. It should be made clear that any unauthorized disclosure of information is illegal and can be subject to prosecution and a fine.

When dealing with children in the context of community theatre and its tactile nature, if, for example, a director wants them to perform in a certain way, it should be explained to them why it is necessary and in all cases the child's consent is required for any physical contact such as holding hands.

What to do if there is a problem

Each society should appoint a child protection officer (CPO) who should naturally be CRB checked and will be the person to whom a child or adult can confidently turn to report any alleged abuse. The CPO will also be the person who liaises with the police and social services. If the CPO is the subject of an accusation of abuse another responsible person, possibly the chairman, should handle such matters.

It should be made clear it is not the society's role or the CPO's job to determine if a child has been abused, but to ensure concerns are shared and appropriate action taken by contacting police and social services. It is important to keep a record of events and also explain to the child what will happen. When talking to the child the CPO must not lead the questioning but merely seek clarification of what the child is saying. It is also important to note that the identity of the accused and accuser must be kept confidential.

Sometimes there may be accidents and any child should be treated by the designated first aider in the presence of the chaperone or CPO. The CPO will have to countersign the written record of the accident and treatment.

A child protection policy is not as complicated or as daunting as it seems. The bottom line is the welfare of a group's younger and vulnerable members. Like health and safety, it is about making a risk assessment regarding potential dangers and seeking to address these. Basically, it is common sense, like having separate dressing rooms, avoiding inappropriate photography, making sure no adult is ever left alone with a child, etc.

NODA publishes an up-to-date fact sheet to help member societies address this important issue.

Case study

Bramley Parish Theatre Players

The Bramley Parish Theatre Players perform their annual pantomime at St Margaret's Church, performing the likes of *Dick Whittington*, *Aladdin*, *Babes in the Wood*, *Robinson Crusoe* and *Puss in Boots*, and drawing on local talent to great success every year. They are the epitome of a community theatre group, encouraging participation from all sections of the Bramley community.

In June 2006 the Players formally adopted a child protection policy (which they revised in December 2006), which they published on their website and of which made all existing and new members aware. They also issued guidelines for rehearsals and performance for the children and young persons in their pantomimes. Sarah Coulson is the group's child protection officer:

'We really started from what we believed to be good practice, with a little help from the NODA website. We have a very experienced child protection team, consisting of a guider, a scouter and the Church of England parish child protection liaison, who also works in education. Our chairman is also a retired teacher. 'We felt that it was important to have a named officer, myself and a back-up team (in case someone had issues with the child protection officer or I wasn't around). This means that for any issues that come up there is a dedicated team to deal with it and support each other. We also felt that it was important for adults to have someone to talk to if they felt that the behaviour of one of our younger members towards them was inappropriate.'

'The practicality of applying our policy also comes down to common sense. We do make sure that all the adults who are working backstage with our cast during productions undergo a brief training with one of the team who is certified to deliver child protection training. We ask that people think carefully about what they say and how they say it, as well as their body language. Also, we make sure (as far as we can) that there are always two adults who arrive at all our rehearsals/shows, preferably either members of the child protection team or other members of the committee, and that there are at least two adults left when all the children have left. We also make sure that that we have parental permission for any photos we take of our younger members for publicity or our website.'

Bramley Parish Theatre Players' Edward Turner reported after their successful 2007 pantomime *Puss In Boots*: 'Child Protection is an issue we have addressed with appropriate training and monitoring. All young people know whom to approach with any issues. They also have representatives on the committee during productions so that they can be heard by those organising and in control. We have active monitoring of our no-photography rule during performances but have made provision for parents to photograph their own children on set if they wish. This was vigorously implemented during the *Puss In Boots* and about three people were requested to delete photos from their camera as our front-of-house staff had seen them taking photos. This has to be done as we have some children who may not be photographed at all. The named photographer knows who must be removed before we use photographs for publicity or on the website, but confidentiality obviously prevents us naming these children to others. A member of the child protection team is at all rehearsals and arrives at least 15 minutes before the start. There is a protocol for dealing with child protection issues – not published for all, but on file and in the hands of those who need it. One parent commented appreciatively and positively about the way we care for children.'

Data protection

Community theatre groups can store basic information about both their members and their audience. In all cases, under the Data Protection Act 1998 consent will be required and an explanation given regarding how this information may or may not be used.

Members

First, with regard to members of a theatre group, it is recommended that a consent clause be signed by all members. This clause would ideally be part of a membership form, including a general explanation to members of what information about them is kept on record and what it is used for.

Basically, to be a member of a group you would divulge your name and contact details (address, telephone number or email address) so that you may be informed, via newsletter, of the group's events. The secretary (and/or membership officer) would handle the information and use it solely for this purpose. In theory, this is the only person who should have access to the information. However, in the course of the society's activities, another member – maybe the director of the next production, or the social secretary of the committee – may need to approach members directly to request help.

The options are to have this as part of the consent clause, and making it explicit to members that they may be contacted directly by a director, or the member may request that all initial communication should be supplied via the secretary. Some groups publish the contact details of their committee, or the cast and crew of a production when it is confirmed, in a newsletter. As long as there is signed consent this should not be a problem.

Other information kept on record about members is their subscription details and whether the subscription is up to date. If your group has children as members or might use children in a future production, another piece of information to be kept on record, with the appropriate documentation, is which members have been CRB checked and could fulfil the roles as chaperones.

In the media

Other information that would probably be in the public domain via theatre programmes, newspapers and the website are members' names and the roles and backstage jobs they have done for the group. This falls in the sphere of publicity, but it is always worth getting consent for all these things. Publicity is part and parcel of theatre, and it is a basic courtesy to make members aware at the outset that they may be required to be part of publicity photographs, interviews and features in the media and online.

On occasions, contact details of a member may need to be made public, for example, a drive for new members may result in a newspaper article where a telephone number of the membership secretary is published. It is important that consent is sought here, and that it is made clear to anyone undertaking such a role in the group that this would be a requirement. Similarly, a press officer for the group should expect his/her telephone details to be passed to media organizations such as local newspapers and local radio. Most groups have a website and neatly sidestep this problem with a generic email link such as membership@ reallygoodcommunitytheatregroup.net or press@reallygood-communitytheatregroup.net. It is important that all this information remains accurate and up to date, particularly if there is a change of personnel.

Audience

With regard to details about individual audience members, where a theatre group may wish to create a database in order to be able to contact the audience directly about future productions, explicit consent from the audience member concerned is needed. Members of the public must be told what information about them will be kept on record: name and address and what publicity material has been sent to them and what it is used for, i.e. marketing. Make clear that this information will not be passed on to third parties. Once the member of the public has signed their consent and confirmed that the details are accurate then they can become part of the group's mailing list for future productions.

The recommendation is to get signed consent from members and audience. By the same token, a member of the group or a member of the public has the right to see what information is held about them and also has the power to have that information removed. For example, a group member may not be comfortable about having their telephone number made available to all members on a cast and crew list, or a member of the public may no longer wish to receive information about productions (it is always worth trying to find out why in this case). In these cases, the group must comply with the request.

The most complicated and sensitive data that a group will have to store relates to disciplinary and complaints procedures. Record-keeping here is essential if there is a complaint about a member. A group should have a disciplinary procedure in place, which may include verbal and written warnings against a member. In this case, check the legal position – the member may not want such information kept on record while it may be prudent for the group to retain the information for a given amount of time.

NODA and other similar organizations have up-to-date information and advice which member societies can source.

Disciplinary and grievance procedures

There are, unfortunately, occasions when there are complaints made against a member or members of a society, with which the group has to deal. There may be complaints made by the public about members of the group, or the complaints may stem from members themselves about other members within the group. Certain procedures and measures need to be in place to deal with errant members. What follows is a guide, but ultimately each group must decide on their own system of disciplinary and grievance procedures.

With any rule enforcement there need to be written rules in the first place. Your group will need to establish what behaviour constitutes misconduct and gross misconduct. It will need to establish a disciplinary committee and decide what sanctions can be imposed against an errant member. There will also need to be a procedure and time frame for such a process. All this needs to be formally laid down in writing and available to all members.

Misconduct

This is behaviour that a group deems unacceptable, such as persistent lateness, unauthorized absence, failure to meet known work standards, smoking in non-smoking areas, misuse of props, etc. Examples of this can be found during the rehearsal stage. Rehearsal schedules are drawn up by the director and production manager specifically to accommodate actors' other commitments, such as work, holidays, etc. An actor's unauthorized absence can seriously disrupt the rehearsal as it affects their fellow cast members and potentially has a knock-on effect on the rehearsal process and, in the worst-case scenario, the performance.

Stand-ins in rehearsals, through no fault of their own, are never satisfactory. They have to read from the script, probably unaware of the established moves, and deliver the lines in a different way from the cast actor. Although everyone else is working on the scene it is unlikely to progress smoothly or effectively. Any developments or changes made at this stage have to be run through again with the missing actor in a later rehearsal.

Most societies are very explicit about unauthorized absences. If an actor is absent for two or three rehearsals, for example, that actor may be punished by being dropped from the cast and replaced with another actor. This can have a knock-on effect in the future for the unfortunate actor if no adequate explanation is forthcoming. Future directors will be reluctant to cast someone who is regarded as unreliable. Reliability is very important in community theatre because everyone is dependent upon everyone else.

Wallace Wareham, Newmarket Operatic, Musical and Dramatic Society's Youth Group leader at the King's Theatre, recalled: 'We were doing one show and were in the late stage of the rehearsals when we got a call from a boy saying his dad was taking him away on holiday and he'd be away for some of the performances. I had no option but to tell him he couldn't be in it, which didn't go down well with him or his parents. You can't allow that to happen. I explained to him that his absence would let down his fellow cast members on the shows he wasn't there for and would be noticed by the audience. It is a commitment and you have to stick to it.'

Gross misconduct

There are other types of behaviour that can be deemed so serious and reflect so badly upon the group that instant dismissal is the necessary option. This type of gross misconduct could be potentially criminal in nature, such as violence, abuse, assault, theft, fraud, drug taking and being drunk. On occasions, it may be necessary to inform the relevant authorities such as the police or social services.

The disciplinary committee needs to deal severely with the perpetrator of any type of behaviour that can be deemed potentially dangerous to fellow members or members of the public. Acts that deliberately breach health and safety procedures are the sort of behaviour that warrants action against the errant member.

Procedure

1 Oral warning – formally given and recorded (minor offence).
2 First written warning – formally given and recorded (subsequent minor offences or serious offence); remains in force for six months.

3 Final written warning – states warning and consequences of further misconduct; remains in force for at least a year.
4 Suspension or demotion – formally given in writing, with explanation and explicit warning of dismissal.
5 Dismissal – formally given in writing, with explanation.

With any procedure it is very important that everything is recorded in writing and copies passed to all relevant parties. There are data protection issues here about confidentiality, particularly for very serious cases, until the issues are resolved.

It is worth noting, however, that it is your society. Who you choose to have as a member is entirely up to you. Provided that any exclusion is not due to discrimination based on race, sex or disability, your group is entitled not to accept the renewal of membership of an individual at annual subscription time. The very nature of having a membership audition, which many musical societies as well youth and dramatic groups do, means there is a selection policy on the basis of talent or potential talent (or lack thereof) in determining who is a member.

Ultimately, any disciplinary matter will have to be resolved by the community theatre group and its members. While outside organizations such as NODA can help you set up a disciplinary and grievance procedure, they cannot become directly involved in any dispute. Although drawing up such a set of rules and procedures may be daunting, it is advisable to do so – just in case. Hopefully, however, you will never have to use it.

Alcohol licensing

The Licensing Act 2003, which is applicable only in England and Wales, introduced changes that affected community theatre groups with regard to entertainment and alcohol licensing.

Community theatre groups that hire a theatre are not affected in anyway, but those groups that own their own theatres or perform in village and/or school halls need to comply with the act. Applications for both entertainment and alcohol must be made to the appropriate local authority.

There are now essentially two types of licence available to community theatre groups who perform in village halls and/or wish to sell alcohol. There is a full premises licence or there is a 'temporary event notice', which covers 'regulated entertainment' (i.e. theatre) and the sale of alcohol.

Temporary event notice

The temporary event notice restricts any event to 96 hours' or four days' duration, which means no production can run for more than four days in a village hall. Coupled with this is the fact that village halls can only be issued with a maximum of 12 temporary event notices a year, totalling up to 15 days a year with at least 24 hours between each event. A group could apply for two notices but, disappointingly, could not run them consecutively.

Full premises licence

The alternative is to get the village hall committee to apply for a full premises licence. This is the more expensive option since the initial main licence fee ranges from £100 to £635 based on the rateable value of the village hall. There is a subsequent annual charge starting at £70 and peaking at £350 based on the same rate. The best course here is for the theatre group to offer to contribute – along with other village hall users – to the licence and the subsequent annual charge.

Personal licence

Where alcohol is on sale, someone from the village hall or the drama group will need to get a personal licence. In order to get this, an accredited qualification is needed (for which fees need to be paid) and, after they have been CRB checked, the person can be appointed the designated premises supervisor, which allows the venue to sell alcohol without the need for a temporary event notice. However, if the sale of alcohol is an income stream for the drama group then arrangements with the village hall committee will be required to agree on profit sharing from such sales.

If you do sell alcohol it is worth noting what type and brand of alcohol is likely to sell. A village hall is not likely to store unsold alcohol on the premises for the next event as it has a significant impact on the hall's insurance.

The benefit of a full premises licence means there would be no restrictions on the run of a production or the number of events at the venue. Furthermore, a person with a personal licence can authorize up to 50 events (maximum of 12 per venue) in a year at other venues (useful if the group wants to do a local tour) in the local authority's statutory area and the licence is valid for ten years.

Venue-owning community theatre groups

Community theatre groups who own their own theatres must have a full premises licence to sell alcohol and host 'regulated entertainment'. There needs to be a personal licence holder who will become the designated premises supervisor for the venue to allow this to happen.

School halls

If the school has a purpose-built theatre, which hosts both professional and amateur productions, then it will be subject to full premises licensing. If, however, the school hires out its hall on an occasional basis to amateur theatre groups and other community events, then it should be able to benefit from the free licensing for public entertainment under the Act for 'village halls, community halls or other similar buildings.' Sale of alcohol, however, would continue to be subject to obtaining a temporary event notice unless the school is willing to obtain a full premises licence or the local authority is prepared to apply for a full premises licence on behalf of the school.

Scotland

In Scotland the Licensing (Scotland) Act 2005 only impacts on the sale of alcohol. Community theatre groups can apply for up to four occasional licences for periods of four or more days or they can apply for up to 12 occasional licences for events up to four days. Either way, the maximum coverage is 56 days in a calendar year. The applications in Scotland have to be submitted to the Chief Constable and the Licensing Standards Officer.

Portrayal of race

It is fair to say that, generally speaking, community theatre is a predominantly white affair. Down the years many community theatre groups have tried and failed to attract potential members from ethnic minorities. Community theatre groups do have an open-door policy but despite this the hobby has remained largely middle class and white.

This can present a problem when plays and musicals feature characters from ethnic backgrounds. Historically, amateur groups have utilized stage make-up, for example, to turn a white actor into a black character using black stage make-up in a practice termed 'blacking up'. Nowadays such a practice has been deemed largely unacceptable. This has presented a problem for societies who wish to stage such productions such as *Show Boat*, *Ragtime* and *South Pacific*, which feature principal and supporting ethnic characters, so community theatre groups have run into problems.

Productions of *Showboat* by Teeside Operatic Society, Glenrothes Amateur Musical Association and Studley Operatic Society were banned by Middlesbrough Town Council, Fife Council and Redditch Borough Council respectively over the issue. The councils owned the venues in which the societies were going to perform. Studley OS, a 45-strong all-white society at the time, sidestepped the ban by switching from the council-owned Palace Theatre in Redditch to the amateur volunteer-run Norbury Theatre in Droitwich. In Glenrothes AMA's case a compromise was reached with Fife Council with the use of 'sympathetic brown make-up'.

Rotherham Council became the first council to produce a formal written policy on the issue, which was imposed on all their buildings and led to Rotherham Operatic Society being unable to stage *South Pacific* at the Civic Theatre.

The reality is that councils may have a formal or informal policy on the matter and they have to comply with and promote the Race Relations (Amendment) Act 2000. Societies wishing to stage such productions but that have insufficient ethnic minority actors on which to draw need to talk to their local authorities to see if there is a possibility of staging it. Certainly the right holders would refuse the staging of an overtly all-white cast when race is such an intrinsic part of the story.

In 1999 Josef Weinberger Limited, the agents for the Rodgers & Hammerstein Organization, published a casting policy on their behalf with regard to *Show Boat* in which it stated:

> 'Where it has been impossible to comply with the author's casting requirements, the practice has arisen where white actors have portrayed the black characters. While this practice is not condoned... we have been granted discretion to allow our licensees to cast the show based on the procedures acceptable to the specific community in which the show is being performed.'

The policy emphasizes that consultation with the relevant local authorities, venue managements and local black community is required to make sure no offence is caused by the portrayal of black characters by white actors.

'It is a difficult issue because quite clearly in certain rural communities it may be difficult to cast exactly as the play is written. However, that is no excuse in some urban communities where effort could be made to engage with people from ethnic communities, as has been done successfully by some groups...

'The problem with blacking up is the use of make-up to represent people of a different race. It is not just about people finding it offensive, some people find it ludicrous. So NODA has a fact sheet that explains the background and sets out a compromise position which is all about talking to each other and understanding each other's point of view.

'There will be circumstances where, with dignity and sensitivity, some people may be able to represent characters from ethnic minorities perhaps, but make-up should never be used to reinforce a stereotype.'

Mark Pemberton, NODA Chief Executive

However, there have been community theatre groups who have consciously sought to source appropriate actors for the parts and regard the problem as no different from sourcing any other type of actor for a particular part.

Case study

West Bromwich Operatic Society: *Ragtime – The Musical*

West Bromwich Operatic Society was formed in 1939. It is a musical society that performs to the highest standard and has earned a reputation that saw it recommended as of the first amateur societies in the country to perform *The Witches of Eastwick*.

In 2004, West Bromwich OS decided to stage *Ragtime*, a musical that includes a number of black characters, at the Grand Theatre in Wolverhampton. The society's business manager, Edward Matty, was given the task of sourcing black actors for the parts.

'It was a struggle. We approached a number of local black organizations such as gospel singers, but were quite surprised at the lack of interest with a mixture of polite and curt rejections.

The local press were reluctant to help because it was perceived as a sensitive issue,' recalled Edward.

The society then printed leaflets and targeted areas where potential black actors could be found. The leaflet explained the show but made a selling point of the fact that the actors would have the opportunity to perform on the Grand Theatre stage. These leaflets produced a response and an interest from a number of potential actors. However, once an initial commitment had been made West Bromwich OS was disappointed that the actors were not turning up.

Edward and his team were persistent and followed up with phone calls to all who had expressed an interest. The lead actor needed five or six approaches before he became fully involved.

'The point was, the man had work commitments and we were asking him to come out of his comfort zone – just like any other new member, irrespective of skin colour. He didn't realize what was involved but once he was he absolutely loved it. We didn't have just one or two new black actors, which may have been hard for them, but had a large group which made it easier for them all to bond and mix.'

The lead actor loved the experience so much he ended up performing *Ragtime* with a number of different societies who had seen his excellent performance in the West Bromwich OS production.

West Bromwich OS doesn't support the policy of staging musicals to fit the existing membership but advocates staging the musicals they want to do irrespective of the potential casting problems that may arise. The problems of attracting new members are a general problem and not specific to the black community.

'It is about attracting new people to try something they have never done before and come out of their comfort zone,' explained Edward.

Disappointingly, only one of the black actors from *Ragtime* remained a regular member but others have come and gone in the interim. Retention of new members is a problem across amateur theatre since there are so many other attractions, as well as the commitments of people's domestic and working lives, which can also present obstacles.

Case study

Orpheus Club: *Show Boat*

In 2001, the Orpheus Club of Glasgow staged *Show Boat* at the Theatre Royal. Director Walter Paul and the OC's committee had no intention of 'blacking up', despite the dearth of black actors within their membership. In fact, they had never had any black members and only two Asian members.

The OC contacted Glasgow City Council and the Race Relations Unit who put them in touch with local black and Asian cultural groups. It was a slow-moving process but, helped by a series of local newspaper articles, the OC was able to cast a chorus of 12 black performers alongside 43 white performers and, more importantly, cast black actors as Joe and Queenie. Another benefit was permission to include the rarely performed misery scene, utilizing the black chorus and also a deeper understanding of the language in the script.

It was an impressive achievement considering Glasgow, according to the 1991 census, boasted only 711 black Africans, 217 black Caribbeans, and 711 in other black groups, but not impossible. Compare that with the number of white members in a major urban town or city.

In an article in *NODA National News*, Walter Paul wrote: 'Plan ahead, announce you intend to produce it, and prepare. If you can't present correctly, then don't do it.'

glossary

Theatre, like everything else, has developed its own vocabulary. Below is a basic glossary to help you through the world of community theatre.

actor/actress A person who performs a character, speaking or non-speaking, in a play.

ad-lib That moment when an actor has forgotten his next line but continues on regardless. It can look seamless if you're good at it but if not... don't think about it.

advance bar A lighting bar which is hung over the auditorium.

amplifier (amp) An electronic device used to increase the strength of a current or sound signal, that is, makes things louder and clearer.

apron The part of the stage that sticks out in front of the proscenium arch.

arena theatre A theatre with an almost 'in the round' performance area, for example, Sheffield's Crucible Theatre and Chichester's Festival Theatre.

aside A line deliberately directed at the audience but not heard by the other characters.

audition Trying out for a role in a play or musical or community theatre group.

auditorium The area in the theatre where the audience sits.

bar Usually made of metal and from which lighting and other equipment may be suspended. (Also popular place where cast and crew go to have a drink and let their hair down!)

barn doors Flaps on the side of a lantern spotlight that can determine the spread of the beam.

batten A length of wood used to reinforce scenery *or* a row of stage-lights.

beginner's call Five minutes before curtain-up, so all actors needed at the start of the play should be in position to begin.

blackout At the end of a scene, act or play when all the lights go out (except for the discreet lighting of the exits).

blacks Plain black drapes sometimes used instead of scenery *or* black clothing used by stage crew when moving props and scenery between scenes in a blackout.

blocking The director's instructions to actors on stage as to who goes where, when and how *or* when the audience's view of an actor on stage is obscured.

book, the With reference to musicals the libretto is known as 'the book'.

Book, the The master script invariably kept by the stage manager to which all should adhere. It is the bible of the production.

boom A vertical metal tube from which lighting equipment may be hung.

border Strips of fabric that conceal the technical equipment from view and frame the top of the stage.

break a leg 'Good Luck' when speaking to someone before a show in which they are involved, but nobody really knows why this expression is used!

calls Time-keeping for actors, usually given by the stage manager who may give a 'quarter-hour' and 'five-minute' call before the show begins. However, this is merely a courtesy service and it is up to the actor to be where he/she should be on time and be responsible for the consequences if he/she is not!

chase Programmed sequence lighting.

chorus The non-principal actors in a musical, or a group of people telling the story in classical theatre, i.e. Greek, Roman and occasionally Shakespearean.

circle The balcony seating in a theatre.

corpse The unforgivable sin of an actor giggling or laughing unscripted during a performance.

costume Whatever an actor wears on stage.

cross-fade Transition from one lighting effect to another.

cue A line spoken or piece of action that takes place just before an actor's own line/appearance.

cue-lights Low-wattage single blue-bulb flashlight signal given by stage manager to an actor who is unable to see his/her non-verbal cue to enter.

curtain (tabs) The front curtain of a proscenium arch theatre. It is colloquially called 'tabs' as actors used to freeze and create a tableau as the curtain came down.

cyclorama (cyc) Cloth that has been stretched and used as a backdrop upon which coloured lighting and/or projected images can be transmitted.

dark When a theatre has no performances to offer and is closed to the public.

dimmer A device that controls the brightness of the stage lights.

director The man or woman who is responsible for the overall creative output of a play.

DLP (dead letter perfect) When an actor knows all his/her lines accurately.

downstage The part of the stage that is closest to the audience.

dress rehearsal (the dress) A fully-fledged performance (run-through) without interruption but not in front of an audience. Usually takes place on the eve of the show's opening.

dressing room Where actors become characters by changing into their costume and applying appropriate stage make-up.

dry When an actor forgets his/her lines either in rehearsal or, God forbid, in performance.

end stage A room where the stage is at one end with the audience facing it.

equalisation (EQ) The creation of the tone of the sound. (Look at your Hi-Fi!)

eye line What the character sees in front of him/her and the audience believe he/she is seeing.

fader Controls sound and/or lighting levels.

flat A canvas-covered wooden frame which is then painted to create scenery.

flies The space above a conventional proscenium arch stage.

floats Footlights.

flood Stage lanterns that flood an area with light.

flown scenery Scenery which can be pulled up and down.

flying When an actor, wearing a concealed harness, is hauled through the air on 'invisible' wires to simulate flying.

fly tower A space where full-sized flats can be erected.

follow spot The stage light that highlights and follows a particular performer, most often used in musicals.

footlights Lighting at the front of the stage.

fourth wall Where the audience sits in a typical proscenium arch theatre, but to the actors it is the other wall in the room and they don't acknowledge the presence of the audience.

fresnel A stage light that gives a soft, unfocused beam.

front of house (FOH) The public area of a theatre.

gauze Stage cloth that can be opaque (if lit from the front) or semi-transparent (if lit from the back).

gel Plastic sheet (that comes in many different colours) that is inserted into the front of a stage light to produced the desired coloured light on stage.

get-in When a theatre group (or company) takes over the theatre for their production.

get-out When a theatre group (or company) has to leave the theatre, taking everything with them.

gobo A disc made of metal or glass that is inserted into a stage light to project an image or pattern on stage that has been etched out or painted on the metal or glass.

gods The audience seats or standing area on the highest balcony of a theatre.

grid The framework from which lighting and scenery bars are hung above stage (most obviously seen at rock concerts).

groundrow Low scenery placed on a stage.

ground plan The designer's scale model of the production design to which the full set will be copied.

half, the Half an hour before 'beginner's call' (or 35 minutes before curtain-up), when all actors should be at the theatre for a performance.

house What actors call the audience, usually in the context of how many bums are on seats for a particular performance!

improvisation Unscripted drama which effectively is made-up as you go along.

intelligent lighting (wigglies) Remotely controlled lighting that can have its position changed during a performance.

iris A device that can vary the size of a beam from a profile stage light.

iron A fire curtain. These have to be tested at least once when an audience is present, with the test usually taking place during the interval.

ladder Another type of frame (it looks like a ladder!) from which lights can be hung vertically.

lamp The bulb in a stage lantern.

lantern Stage light.

leg Material, usually in vertical strips, that blocks the view of the audience into the wings.

light curtain A wall of light created by parcans (see below).

lighting Anything to do with illuminating or lighting the stage in a particular way.

lighting desk Desk at which the lighting technician enacts the lighting cues.

mark out In rehearsal, without the benefit of the actual set, the set's dimensions and furniture is marked out on the floor.

mask When you hide something from the audience's view (either deliberately or unintentionally). Of course, it can be just a mask worn by an actor/character!

matinée A daytime performance, usually in the afternoon.

melodrama (melodramatic) Seen as unconvincing displays of emotion.

method acting A style of acting where the actor uses his/her own 'emotional memory' to attain the character's 'emotional truth'.

microphone (mic) The device that helps to increase the volume of an actor's or singer's voice.

mute The suppressing of all sound.

noise boy Sound engineer.

off the book When an actor knows his/her lines sufficiently to dispense with the script in their hands during rehearsal. A pleasing sight for any director.

open white (O/W) A gel-free stage light.

opposite prompt (OP) Stage right.

parcan Stage light that produces an oval parallel beam.

perches Lighting fixed to or just behind the proscenium arch.

plot List of technical cues for sound, lighting and special effects *or* a play's storyline.

principal Actor in a leading role in a musical.

producer A director of a musical.

profile A stage light with lens (or lenses) to clearly define the beam.

promenade A type of theatre where the audience moves to a different location for each scene.

prompt (prompter) A person who sits in the wings stage left during a performance, ready to feed an actor the correct line if he/she should 'dry'. Ideally should not be heard or needed.

properties (props) Anything used by an actor on stage during the performance.

proscenium arch (proscenium)   A picture-framed end stage.

public address (PA) Equipment for amplifying sound.

pyrotechnics Special effects on stage that result in bangs, smoke, flashes or flames.

raked stage (rake) A stage that slightly slopes from back to front towards the audience – hence upstage and downstage – to enhance audience sight lines.

scene The part of a play portraying a particular time and/or location within the story.

scenery Anything that creates the environment of a scene.

script The play or musical in its written and printed form.

set The stage environment in which a play is performed.

setting line An invisible line at the back of the stage that depicts the base line for the building of the set.

shutters Metal blades in profile stage lighting that are utilized to change the dimensions of the beam.

sight lines (lines of sight) What members of the audience see from their seat's position in the theatre. The director and set designer need to be very aware of these.

soliloquy The innermost thoughts of a single character spoken on stage addressing the audience.

sound Any music or audio effect to be heard by the audience during a performance.

stage The performance area of the production.

stage braces A bracket hooked to a flat (see above) to help keep it upright.

stage business Any expressive movement or handling of props is sometimes called 'stage business'.

stage directions Action that is explicitly written in the script by the playwright or informed by the director during rehearsals.

stage left On an actor's left side as he/she stands on the stage looking out to the audience.

stage manager A person of authority and responsibility for all the practical aspects of a performance.

stage right On an actor's right side as he/she stands on the stage looking out to the audience.

stage weights Blocks of solid metal used to stop flats (see above) wobbling.

stalls The lowest level of seating in an auditorium.

state Variable brightness of a fixed pattern of lights.

strike To take down scenery and remove the set from the stage.

tab warmers The lighting of the front curtains before and after the show.

tabs (tableau curtains) See *curtains*.

theatre-in-the-round A type of theatre performance where the audience surrounds the acting area.

thespian Derived from Thespis, the ancient Greek who broke out of the chorus to create a solo spot and, therefore, invented acting. Everyone who followed thus became a thespian.

thrust Where the audience is on three of the four sides of the acting area or part of the stage that extends outward.

tilt Where a light's beam can be moved up or down by rotation.

tormentor A piece of scenery placed between the edge of the set and the proscenium frame to reduce the width of the stage picture.

trap A trap door.

traverse Where the audience occupies only two opposite sides of the acting area.

upstage The area of stage which is furthest away from the audience.

wardrobe Refers to everything to do with costume.

wings The areas either side of the stage which should not be seen by members of the audience.

wipe A single curtain that is drawn completely across the stage.

NODA was founded in 1899 'to protect and advance the interests of Operatic and Dramatic Arts, and of societies engaged therein'. It now has 2,500 members.

Aims:

- To give a shared voice to the amateur theatre sector.
- To help amateur societies and individuals achieve the highest standards of best practice and performance.
- To provide leadership and advice to enable the amateur theatre sector to tackle the challenges and opportunities of the 21st century.

Benefits for members

Advice and Legal Service – providing free expert advice and fact sheets on issues such as setting up a new society, performance regulations and copyright, health and safety, fundraising, child protection and children in theatrical performances, licensing, model constitution for societies (approved by the Charity Commission and Inland Revenue), and model contract for directors. NODA also offers a counter-signatory service for applications for criminal record disclosures.

Representation – to government, funding agencies, local authorities, rights holders and the media.

Conferences, workshops and seminars at national and regional level, to help share information on best practice.

Amateur Theatre Week – annual events to raise the profile of amateur theatre in the national and local media.

Summer School – annual residential event offering training from professional tutors in drama performance, music directing, musical theatre, stage management and other courses for performers, directors and technicians.

Magazines – regular regional magazines and national quarterly magazine featuring a range of useful advice and information for amateur societies and practitioners as well as free listings of performances, free classified ads for selling, buying or hiring scenery, props, scripts, etc. and details of shows released or restricted for amateur performance.

Email newsletter – every month and access to members' area of the NODA website.

Programme and poster competitions at regional and national level.

Contact details

National Operatic and Dramatic Association
NODA House
58–60 Lincoln Road
Peterborough PE1 2RZ
Tel: 0870 770 2480
Fax: 0870 770 2490
www.noda.org.uk

taking it further

Useful contacts

United Kingdom

These websites have a wealth of information and can certainly point you in the right direction on almost every subject concerning community theatre.

Amateur Dramatics and Operatics Dot Com: **www.amadrama.co.uk**

Amdram: **www.amdram.co.uk** – this is the free website for the amateur theatre community and includes free resources for groups and individuals interested in amateur theatre.

Association of Irish Musical Societies: **www.aims.ie**

British Theatre Guide: **www.britishtheatreguide.info**

National Operatic and Dramatic Association: **www.noda.org.uk**

National Operatic and Dramatic Association, North West: **www.nodanw.co.uk**

National Operatic and Dramatic Association, Scotland: **www.nodascotland.co.uk**

The Greater Manchester Drama Festival: **www.gmdf.org**

The Little Theatre Guild: **www.littletheatreguild.org**

The Scottish Community Theatre Association: **www.scda.org.uk**

The Stage: **www.thestage.co.uk**

UK Theatre Web: **www.uktw.com**

What's On Stage: **www.whatonstage.com**

United States

American Association of Community Theatre: **www.aact.org**

The American Association of Community Theatre (AACT) is the national voice of community theatre, representing the interests of community theatres across the USA and with the armed forces overseas – and the individuals who support them. AACT also offers a wide range of member benefits and services.

Address: American Association of Community Theatre, 8402 BriarWood Cr, Lago Vista, TX78645.

Australia

The Association of Community Theatre: **www.showline.com.au**

The Association of Community Theatre is Australia's largest non-profit theatre umbrella organization, with member clubs in all states of Australia. The website provides an events list, photos, a costume and prop register, audition information, a guest book and more.

Canada

International Association of Theatre for Children and Young People: **www.assitejcanada.org**

Books

Here are some books that will allow you to explore different aspects of community theatre further, although this is by no means a comprehensive list.

Actors/acting

Ultimately acting is a doing activity and you will only learn the various aspects of it by doing it and learning from others. The books listed below are both accessible and practical.

Care of the Professional Voice by D. Garfield Davies and Anthony F. Jahn (A & C Black, 2004)

Actor's Guide to Auditions and Interviews by Margo Annett (A & C Black, 2004)

Clear Speech by Malcolm Morrison (Heinemann Publishing, 2007)

So You Want To Be An Actor? by Prunella Scales and Timothy West (Nick Hern Books, 2005)

Stage management

Any or all of these will help you to become an excellent stage manager.

Essentials of Stage Management by Peter Maccoy (A & C Black, 2004)

The ABC of Stage Technology by Francis Reid (A & C Black, 2001)

The Complete Stage Planning Kit by Gillian Davies (A & C Black, 2003)

The Backstage Guide to Stage Management (edition 2) by Thomas A. Kelly (Watson-Guptill, 2004)

Stage Management by Gail Pallon (Nick Hern Books, 2003)

Props

Top tips to make convincing props for the stage.

Stage Source Book: Props by Gill Davies (A & C Black, 2004)

Making Stage Props by Andy Wilson (Crowood Press, 2003)

Theatre design

For beginners, these two books are excellent accessible for anything to do with set.

Stage Source Book: Sets by Gill Davies (A & C Black, 2004)

From Page To Stage by Rosemary Ingham (Heinemann Publishing, 1998)

Director/directing

These books give you and insight into directing for which, I might add, you need absolutely no qualifications, so take good advice where you find it.

Directing Amateur Theatre by Helen E. Sharman (A & C Black, 2004)

Directing A Play by Michael McCaffrey (Phaidon Press, 1988)

Directing Drama by John Miles-Brown (Peter Owen Ltd, 1994)

So You Want To Be A Theatre Director? by Stephen Unwin (Nick Hern Books, 2004)

The Crafty Art of Playmaking by Alan Ayckbourn (Faber and Faber, 2002)

Lighting

Stage Lighting by Graham Walters (A & C Black, 1997)

Lighting The Stage by Francis Reid (A & C Black, 2001)

Sound

A Beginner's Guide To Stage Sound by Peter Coleman (Entertainment Technology Press, 2003)

Theatre Sound by John A. Leonard (A& C Black, 2001)

Wardrobe

Costumes for the Stage by Sheila Jackson (New Amsterdam Press 2001)

More Costumes for the Stage by Sheila Jackson (New Amsterdam Press, 2001)

Make-up

The Actor's Complete Step-By-Step Guide To Today's Techniques and Materials by Laura Thidium (Backstage Books, 1995)

Musicals

Pantomime – A Practical Guide by Tina Bicat with Ruth Staines & Colin Winslow (Crowood Press, 2004)

Producing Musicals by John Gardyne (Crowood Press, 2004)

Staging Youth Theatre by Rex Doyle (Crowood Press, 2004)

•

teach® yourself

From Advanced Sudoku to Zulu, you'll find everything you need in the **teach yourself** range, in books, on CD and on DVD.

Visit **www.teachyourself.co.uk** for more details.

Advanced Sudoku and Kakuro
Afrikaans
Alexander Technique
Algebra
Ancient Greek
Applied Psychology
Arabic
Aromatherapy
Art History
Astrology
Astronomy
AutoCAD 2004
AutoCAD 2007
Ayurveda
Baby Massage and Yoga
Baby Signing
Baby Sleep
Bach Flower Remedies
Backgammon
Ballroom Dancing
Basic Accounting
Basic Computer Skills
Basic Mathematics
Beauty
Beekeeping
Beginner's Arabic Script
Beginner's Chinese Script
Beginner's Dutch

Beginner's French
Beginner's German
Beginner's Greek
Beginner's Greek Script
Beginner's Hindi
Beginner's Italian
Beginner's Japanese
Beginner's Japanese Script
Beginner's Latin
Beginner's Mandarin Chinese
Beginner's Portuguese
Beginner's Russian
Beginner's Russian Script
Beginner's Spanish
Beginner's Turkish
Beginner's Urdu Script
Bengali
Better Bridge
Better Chess
Better Driving
Better Handwriting
Biblical Hebrew
Biology
Birdwatching
Blogging
Body Language
Book Keeping
Brazilian Portuguese

Bridge
British Empire, The
British Monarchy from Henry VIII, The
Buddhism
Bulgarian
Business Chinese
Business French
Business Japanese
Business Plans
Business Spanish
Business Studies
Buying a Home in France
Buying a Home in Italy
Buying a Home in Portugal
Buying a Home in Spain
C++
Calculus
Calligraphy
Cantonese
Car Buying and Maintenance
Card Games
Catalan
Chess
Chi Kung
Chinese Medicine
Christianity
Classical Music
Coaching
Cold War, The
Collecting
Computing for the Over 50s
Consulting
Copywriting
Correct English
Counselling
Creative Writing
Cricket
Croatian
Crystal Healing
CVs
Czech
Danish
Decluttering
Desktop Publishing
Detox

Digital Home Movie Making
Digital Photography
Dog Training
Drawing
Dream Interpretation
Dutch
Dutch Conversation
Dutch Dictionary
Dutch Grammar
Eastern Philosophy
Electronics
English as a Foreign Language
English for International Business
English Grammar
English Grammar as a Foreign Language
English Vocabulary
Entrepreneurship
Estonian
Ethics
Excel 2003
Feng Shui
Film Making
Film Studies
Finance for Non-Financial Managers
Finnish
First World War, The
Fitness
Flash 8
Flash MX
Flexible Working
Flirting
Flower Arranging
Franchising
French
French Conversation
French Dictionary
French Grammar
French Phrasebook
French Starter Kit
French Verbs
French Vocabulary
Freud
Gaelic

Gardening
Genetics
Geology
German
German Conversation
German Grammar
German Phrasebook
German Verbs
German Vocabulary
Globalization
Go
Golf
Good Study Skills
Great Sex
Greek
Greek Conversation
Greek Phrasebook
Growing Your Business
Guitar
Gulf Arabic
Hand Reflexology
Hausa
Herbal Medicine
Hieroglyphics
Hindi
Hindi Conversation
Hinduism
History of Ireland, The
Home PC Maintenance and
   Networking
How to DJ
How to Run a Marathon
How to Win at Casino Games
How to Win at Horse Racing
How to Win at Online Gambling
How to Win at Poker
How to Write a Blockbuster
Human Anatomy & Physiology
Hungarian
Icelandic
Improve Your French
Improve Your German
Improve Your Italian
Improve Your Spanish
Improving Your Employability

Indian Head Massage
Indonesian
Instant French
Instant German
Instant Greek
Instant Italian
Instant Japanese
Instant Portuguese
Instant Russian
Instant Spanish
Internet, The
Irish
Irish Conversation
Irish Grammar
Islam
Italian
Italian Conversation
Italian Grammar
Italian Phrasebook
Italian Starter Kit
Italian Verbs
Italian Vocabulary
Japanese
Japanese Conversation
Java
JavaScript
Jazz
Jewellery Making
Judaism
Jung
Kama Sutra, The
Keeping Aquarium Fish
Keeping Pigs
Keeping Poultry
Keeping a Rabbit
Knitting
Korean
Latin
Latin American Spanish
Latin Dictionary
Latin Grammar
Latvian
Letter Writing Skills
Life at 50: For Men
Life at 50: For Women

Life Coaching
Linguistics
LINUX
Lithuanian
Magic
Mahjong
Malay
Managing Stress
Managing Your Own Career
Mandarin Chinese
Mandarin Chinese Conversation
Marketing
Marx
Massage
Mathematics
Meditation
Middle East Since 1945, The
Modern China
Modern Hebrew
Modern Persian
Mosaics
Music Theory
Mussolini's Italy
Nazi Germany
Negotiating
Nepali
New Testament Greek
NLP
Norwegian
Norwegian Conversation
Old English
One-Day French
One-Day French – the DVD
One-Day German
One-Day Greek
One-Day Italian
One-Day Portuguese
One-Day Spanish
One-Day Spanish – the DVD
Origami
Owning a Cat
Owning a Horse
Panjabi
PC Networking for Small
  Businesses

Personal Safety and Self
  Defence
Philosophy
Philosophy of Mind
Philosophy of Religion
Photography
Photoshop
PHP with MySQL
Physics
Piano
Pilates
Planning Your Wedding
Polish
Polish Conversation
Politics
Portuguese
Portuguese Conversation
Portuguese Grammar
Portuguese Phrasebook
Postmodernism
Pottery
PowerPoint 2003
PR
Project Management
Psychology
Quick Fix French Grammar
Quick Fix German Grammar
Quick Fix Italian Grammar
Quick Fix Spanish Grammar
Quick Fix: Access 2002
Quick Fix: Excel 2000
Quick Fix: Excel 2002
Quick Fix: HTML
Quick Fix: Windows XP
Quick Fix: Word
Quilting
Recruitment
Reflexology
Reiki
Relaxation
Retaining Staff
Romanian
Running Your Own Business
Russian
Russian Conversation

Russian Grammar
Sage Line 50
Sanskrit
Screenwriting
Second World War, The
Serbian
Setting Up a Small Business
Shorthand Pitman 2000
Sikhism
Singing
Slovene
Small Business Accounting
Small Business Health Check
Songwriting
Spanish
Spanish Conversation
Spanish Dictionary
Spanish Grammar
Spanish Phrasebook
Spanish Starter Kit
Spanish Verbs
Spanish Vocabulary
Speaking On Special Occasions
Speed Reading
Stalin's Russia
Stand Up Comedy
Statistics
Stop Smoking
Sudoku
Swahili
Swahili Dictionary
Swedish
Swedish Conversation
Tagalog
Tai Chi
Tantric Sex
Tap Dancing
Teaching English as a Foreign
    Language
Teams & Team Working
Thai
Theatre
Time Management
Tracing Your Family History
Training

Travel Writing
Trigonometry
Turkish
Turkish Conversation
Twentieth Century USA
Typing
Ukrainian
Understanding Tax for Small
    Businesses
Understanding Terrorism
Urdu
Vietnamese
Visual Basic
Volcanoes
Watercolour Painting
Weight Control through Diet &
    Exercise
Welsh
Welsh Dictionary
Welsh Grammar
Wills & Probate
Windows XP
Wine Tasting
Winning at Job Interviews
Word 2003
World Cultures: China
World Cultures: England
World Cultures: Germany
World Cultures: Italy
World Cultures: Japan
World Cultures: Portugal
World Cultures: Russia
World Cultures: Spain
World Cultures: Wales
World Faiths
Writing Crime Fiction
Writing for Children
Writing for Magazines
Writing a Novel
Writing Poetry
Xhosa
Yiddish
Yoga
Zen
Zulu